Everything Has Its price

Richard E. Donley

A FIRESIDE BOOK

PUBLISHED BY SIMON & SCHUSTER

New York • London • Toronto

Sydney • Tokyo • Singapore

FIRESIDE
Rockefeller Center
1230 Avenue of the Americas
New York, New York 10020

FIRESIDE and colophon are registered trademarks of Simon &
Schuster Inc.
Designed by Pei Koay
Manufactured in the United States of America

10   9   8   7   6   5   4   3   2   1

Library of Congress Cataloging-in-Publication Data
Donley, Richard.
Everything has its price / Richard Donley.
p.   cm.
"A Fireside book."
1. Shopping—United States—Directories. 2. Consumer
goods—United States—Prices. I. Title.
TX336.D66 1995
380. 1' 45' 0002573 —dc20   94-38526
                                             CIP

ISBN: 0-671-89559-1

contents

Introduction and Acknowledgments

THIS BOOK IS AN ARMCHAIR SHOPPING SPREE.
While not exactly an *indispensable* price guide, it is, hopefully, a compulsively readable one, full of strange and unusual services, and lavish and exorbitant goods; but also full of prices for everyday items (stop signs, phone booths, mannequins et al.) that most of us have occasionally looked at and wondered: How much does one of those cost? Almost everything included here is something you could buy if you had the desire, and, more important, the money. Some are items you aren't likely to need (airplane tires or armored cars), some are things most of us cannot afford (roller coasters, Van Gogh paintings), and some are things we hope not to need anytime soon (a bail bond, coronary bypass surgery, or being buried at sea). But they *can* be purchased. In putting this book together, it didn't take long to realize that, indeed, everything *does* have its price.

Consider this the book equivalent of strolling down Rodeo Drive, or spending a weekend shopping in Manhattan, or browsing through every mouth-watering catalog that has ever been popped into a mailbox. This book is an armchair shopper's version of nirvana.

All the prices included here were obtained from a wide variety of sources: from books, magazines, advertisements, government agencies, and, in most cases, directly from the suppliers or their catalogs. When there was a price range on any given item, the low end of that range was usually selected. In most cases, the "list" price has been used. Sometimes the item can be procured for less. Every effort has been made to ensure that these are the most accurate and up-to-date prices available. Of course, as any good shopper knows, prices for anything, anyplace, at any time are subject to change without notice. Sources are frequently listed just in case readers see something they can't live without.

For their advice, assistance, and encouragement in putting this book together, I would like to take a moment to thank Wayne Bartley, Mabel Beardsley, Austin Belton, John Bennett, Dr. Tom Bird, Peter Borland, Paul Cort, Arland Cottingham, Roy Dentlinger, Vince DiFruscio, Jr., Les Donley, Velma Donley, Jeff Dunn, Dave Feamster, Margaret Fimple, Rhonda Gettel, Lisa Hancock, Bob Hayes, Bridgette Jette, Shirley Klipfel, Joe Klune, John Logsdon, Daniel Martinez, Kevin McCarthy, Harold Moss, Kevin O'Brien, Betty O'Donnell, Ed Perry, Vess Quinlan, Cyril Reynaud, Edward Rutledge, Dr. Elizabeth Rutledge, Rod Simpson, Sam Staggs, Bob Vassar, Floreine Wickizer, and the entire (very skilled and helpful) staff at the Pueblo Regional Library.

Special thanks must go to several people without whose help this book might never have seen the light of day: Bob Benvenuto, my editor Becky Cabaza, Jean Eskra, my agent Stephanie Laidman, Leigh W. Rutledge, and Charlotte Simmons. Of course, I take full responsibility for any of the book's shortcomings and for any errors that may have crept into the manuscript.

Unfortunately, it is not possible to mention by name the hundreds of people at the dozens of companies, associations, and government agencies who gave willingly of their time to dispense helpful information.

Finally, I would enjoy hearing from anyone who has comments, additions, corrections, questions, or even complaints about this book. Those so inclined should write to:

Richard E. Donley
P.O. Box 1198
Key West FL, 33041–1198

In the Name of Love

It may be impossible to put a price tag on love, but where love is concerned price is often no object. What else can explain a $1,200 wedding cake or a $16,000 personal "Cybersex" machine?

25-word personals ad in the *New York Review of Books:*   **$78.75**

$3.15 per word, with a 15-word minimum. Where the well-read seek their counterparts for love and romance.
Source: *New York Review of Books*, 250 West 57th St., New York, NY 10107 (212-257-8070)

8-day "clothes-free" cruise: **$745**

On-board accommodations range from $745 to $1,795 per person. Cruise ship departs from New Orleans for an 8-day western Caribbean itinerary. Bare Necessities Tour & Travel Company—"Providing the Luxury of Deciding What *Not* to Wear"—offers a variety of clothes-free tours and resort packages.

Source: Bare Necessities Tour & Travel Company, 1502 A West Ave., Austin, TX 78701 (512-499-0405)

Private strip-tease lessons (per hour):   **$35**

Source: Marliza's Belly Dance School, Las Vegas, NV (702-870-5508)

Penis enlargement (phalloplasty):   **$2,600**
The procedure involves removing excess fat from one
part of the body, and then injecting it beneath the skin
of the penis. As a result, length can be increased by as
much as an inch, while diameter can be approximately
doubled. However, some of the fat eventually dis-
solves, causing the organ to lose some of its newfound
size.

Vasectomy: **$300**
$300–$350 when done through Planned Parenthood,
about $450 when done by a private physician. The pro-
cedure does not generally require hospitalization.

Having a vasectomy undone: **$880**
The success rate is only about 50%. The longer it's
been since you've had the original vasectomy, the
more difficult it is to reverse.

A female or male prostitute from a   **$150**
Las Vegas escort service (per hour):
Tips are encouraged. Street prostitutes, who operate
with little overhead, are generally a great deal less expensive. In New York, for example, a female prostitute
working in the Hunt's Point section of the Bronx might
provide some sexual services for as little as $5; on
lower Park Avenue, the cost would probably run closer
to $50. Hollywood madam Heidi Fleiss reportedly
billed her call girls out at $1,500 a night—and higher.

License for a legal brothel in Nevada (annual):   **$25,600**
For a brothel with 1 to 20 rooms in Lyon County, just
outside of Carson City, the state capital. Brothels are
legal in twelve Nevada counties, and each county es-
tablishes its own fees. A brothel with 41 or more rooms
would pay $33,600 per year. In addition, anyone ap-
plying for a license must pay an investigation fee of
$2,000 to determine whether they are "morally fit" to
be licensed.

Buying a Nevada brothel:
At any one time, there are usually two or three actively
for sale. The going price is a million and up. A 14-room
brothel in Elko is currently available for about $1.5 mil-
lion—an "excellent buy," according to one expert.
Source: The Nevada Brothel Association, 700 West
Fourth St., Reno, NV 89503 (702-323-1402)

**$1.5
million**

How to Become a Gigolo **(booklet):**
"All the special details for men who want to make a
living being pleasing companions to bored, usually
frustrated, women."
Source: Eden Press, P.O. Box 8410, Fountain Valley, CA
92728 (800-338-8484)

$9

Cybersex "virtual reality" machine:
Though not quite virtual sex, the machine is touted as
the ultimate experience in self-arousal. The Cybersex
machine is equipped with a 486 PC computer with
color monitor, a CD-ROM disk drive that's loaded with
interactive Adults Only software (primarily images of
nude females), and an artificial vagina (it "pulsates,
squeezes, and sucks") that is connected to the computer. The machine can also be connected to a VCR, so
the user can play his own favorite tapes. Unlike other
virtual reality systems, it does not utilize headgear. A
one-time trial of the machine (as opposed to purchas-
ing it) costs $4,000. Thus far, machines have been de-
signed only for men.
Source: Thinking Software, Inc., P.O. Box 770807,
Woodside, NY 11377

$16,000

French maid's uniform (in black leather):
"In this outfit she will feel dainty and pretty and will
serve all your needs." Comes with lace garters and fin-
gerless gloves.
Source: The Pleasure Chest, 7733 Santa Monica Blvd.,
West Hollywood, CA 90046

$79.95

One American black bear gallbladder, $18,000
powdered and processed (in Asia):
The powder is valued in the Far East as an aphrodisiac.

Black rhinoceros horn, powdered and processed: $20,000
Black-market price in Taiwan and Hong Kong. The average horn weighs about 10 kilograms. Like black bear
gallbladder, it is mistakenly believed to be an aphrodisiac in parts of Asia. Though banned by international treaty, the market is fueled by the greed of
poachers. As a result of the continuing slaughter of
these animals, the black rhino population in Africa has
plummeted from 65,000 in 1970 to a staggering 2,000
today.

Sex change operation (female to male): $23,000
Includes mastectomy, hysterectomy, and formation of
penis. Pre-surgery expenses for hormones and psychological counseling are additional.

Sex change operation (male to female): $12,000
Includes genital modification. Implants (if necessary),
as well as hormone therapy and psychological counseling, are additional.

An average American wedding: $19,000
The cost, as calculated by *Forbes* magazine, includes
$2,200 for an engagement ring, $900 for a photogra-
pher, $800 for a wedding gown, $286 for invitations,
and $3,200 for the honeymoon. The single largest ex-
pense is the wedding reception.

Arriving at your wedding in Cinderella's $1,200
glass coach pulled by 6 white ponies:
Includes being attended by costumed footmen. Service
available only for weddings held at Florida's Walt Disney World. Walt Disney World will help design and
execute the "Fantasy Wedding" of your dreams. With
hundreds of options available (such as Cinderella's

coach), the wedding may cost a few thousand dollars—or more than $100,000. The bride or groom can even rent a pair of Mickey Mouse ears to wear during the ceremony.
Source: Walt Disney Attractions, Inc., P.O. Box 10,000, Lake Buena Vista, FL 32830-1000 (407-828-3400)

Gary Hansen wedding cake for 300 people: **$1,200**
For a wedding reception of 300, the famed Los Angeles baker will prepare a five-tier cake of any flavor for $4 per person.
Source: Gary Hansen Cakes, Los Angeles, CA (213-936-5527)

A wedding at "Chapel of the Bells" in Reno: **$99.50**
Reno and Las Vegas are famous for quick and inexpensive weddings. Price includes chapel fee and $35 state marriage license. Flowers and photographs are extra.

A contested divorce in New York City: **$50,000**
Average cost, primarily for legal fees incurred by the wife and husband.

Leg irons: **$29.95**
Available in black metal or chrome.
Source: The Pleasure Chest, 7733 Santa Monica Blvd., West Hollywood, CA 90046

Personal Protection

Life is fraught with danger. But for every peril—toxic chemicals, purse snatchers, megalomaniac rulers bent on world conquest—some clever entrepreneur has tried to come up with an antidote or countermeasure. Personal protection isn't cheap, though. It can cost $60,000 just to protect yourself against a 35-cent bullet fired by an irate motorist in rush-hour traffic.

Bomb shelter: **$24,500**

Base price for the battery-powered ES10 Disaster Shelter, including intruder-proof hatch, air filtration system, toilet, shower, and numerous other features. Affords protection for 10 to 20 people from tornadoes, earthquakes, and chemical and nuclear weapons. According to the distributor, bankers, U.S. representatives, U.S. senators, IRS agents, aerospace/defense contractors, and Middle Eastern countries are the primary purchasers.
Source: The Survival Center, P.O. Box 234, McKenna, WA 98558 (800-321-2900)

6-month emergency food supply for 2 people: **$1,050**

Contains 1,095 freeze- and air-dried meals (packed in nitrogen) providing 2,196 calories and 96 grams of protein per person per day. Meals are ready to eat; no cooking or utensils are required.
Source: The Survival Center, P.O. Box 234, McKenna, WA 98558 (800-321-2900)

Contamination suit: $3,750
The Challenge 6400 vapor protection suit covers the entire body, including the head, is abrasion and flame resistant, and has permeating resistance to over 200 hazardous chemicals. Respirator is extra.
Source: National Draeger, Inc., P.O. Box 120, Pittsburgh, PA 15230-0120

Safer Home Test Kit: $55
Allows the user to test for a variety of household contaminants, including lead, radon, microwave oven radiation, carbon monoxide, and ultraviolet radiation.
Source: Greenpeace (800-916-1616)

Armed bodyguard in Miami (daily rate): $3,000
An unarmed guard costs only $1,500 a day.
Source: CIS, Miami, FL (305-270-1901)

Armor coating for your car: $60,000
The inside of the vehicle is lined with armor, the car's springs are fortified, and bullet-proof glass and non-exploding gas tank are installed. Affords protection against a .44-magnum bullet. For $75,000, a car can be fortified against a 7.62-caliber rifle cartridge. Basic "smash & grab" car protection starts at $8,500.
Source: Bodyguard Armoring, 102 Herrera St., Austin, TX 78742 (800-966-1490)

Tear gas grenade: $23
Source: Central Equipment Co., Millis, MA (508-376-2951)

Brass knuckles "paperweight": $12.95
As advertised in *Soldier of Fortune* magazine.

Lady's handbag equipped with a gun pouch: $44.95
The Side-Kik handbag, made of denim, is the least expensive of thirty gun-toting handbag styles offered by

Feminine Protection of Dallas. Top-of-the-line is the Classic III, made of leather with snakeskin trim ($194.95). The purses also come with a wire built into the shoulder strap to prevent a purse snatcher from cutting it. Feminine Protection sells between 300 and 500 gun-pouched purses a month.
Source: Feminine Protection Inc., 10514 Shady Trail, Dallas, TX 75220 (800-444-7090)

Executive ink pen knife: $4.99
"Looks and works like an ordinary ink pen but pulls apart revealing a 2 ⅝-inch blade." As advertised in *Soldier of Fortune* magazine.

Israeli Uzi submachine gun "counterfeit": $310
An ad in *Soldier of Fortune* magazine claims that these counterfeit guns are "full size working metal models that . . . cannot be fired!" (Similar M-16 assault rifles and Thompson machine guns are also available.)

How to Convert Counterfeit Guns into $12.95
***Working Weapons* (booklet):**

Another ad in *Soldier of Fortune* magazine promises to show you "how to convert the non-firing replica guns into workable and firing weapons."

A year's subscription to *Machine Gun News:* $29.95
"An arsenal of information . . . for the full-auto enthusiast." Copies are mailed with a protective cover "to ensure your privacy."
Source: *Machine Gun News*, P.O. Box 759, Dept. SF01, Hot Springs, AR 71902 (501-623-4951)

Blowgun: $17.99
Fully functional, 2-piece blowgun, made of lightweight black aluminum. A package of 24 wire darts costs $4.99 extra. (Blowguns are illegal in California.)

Source: The Sportsman's Guide, 411 Farwell Ave., South St. Paul, MN 55070-0239 (800-888-3006)

Gunslinger's holster (Old West style): $169.95
The belt is adorned with silver conchos, has 24 molded bullet loops, and is sized to fit your waist and gun.
Source: American Sales & Mfg., Box 677WW, Laredo, TX 78042 (210-723-6893)

Suit of armor (17th century): $80,000
For an *original* and *complete* 17th-century suit of armor. Unfortunately, according to *Forbes* magazine, "experts estimate 70% of all European arms and armor on the market are either reproductions or outright forgeries." In 1983, the auction price for a rare mid-16th-century suit of armor, made for Henry II of France, was $3 million.

Eat, Drink, and Be Merry

A wholesome and delicious Thanksgiving dinner can be put together for under $3 per person. But you can spend $15,000 or more learning how to prepare it properly. Maybe it would just be cheaper to eat out. (Then again, consider what dinner for two would cost at Bouley in New York . . .)

Tuition at The French Culinary Institute (New York City): $15,500

Tuition includes 600 hours of classes (over a 6- to 9-month period) "designed to train the chefs of tomorrow using the classic techniques which are the foundation of contemporary cuisine." Other programs, for the "serious amateur," include the popular 100-hour "Essentials of Pastry" (tuition $2,475, plus a $55 uniform fee). Saturday workshops, on such topics as "Savory Soups" and "Knife Skills," are also offered for $160 per person.

Source: The French Culinary Institute, 462 Broadway, New York, NY 10013-2618 (212-219-8890)

1 dozen chocolate roses: $60

Roses are crafted from milk chocolate, come foil wrapped on a floral stem, and are available through The Chocolate Catalogue from Bissinger's. Bissinger's also offers a 1-pound, solid milk chocolate 12-inch pizza, topped with pecans, coconut, and other sweet morsels ($24).

Source: Karl Bissinger French Confections, 3983 Gratiot Road., St. Louis, MO 63110 (800-325-8881)

Dinner for two at Ginza Sushi Ko in Los Angeles: $400
Reputed to be the most expensive restaurant in Los
Angeles, and a favorite of Madonna, Marlon Brando,
and other celebrities, Ginza Sushi Ko offers sushi cre-
ated from fish flown in twice a week from Tokyo.
("California fish has no taste," proprietor Masa
Takayama once told a reporter.) The restaurant is
renowned not only for the quality of its food but for its
striking presentation of meals as well. The restaurant
does not advertise nor is the exterior marked; it relies
on its reputation for customers. Dinner for two can
run as low as $250, depending on what's ordered.
Price does not include wine.

Dinner for one on the Eiffel Tower: $88
Three-course meal at the restaurant Le Jules Verne, a
third of the way up the Eiffel Tower, at the second platform. Includes a bottle of the house wine, all taxes and
gratuities. Regarded as one of the most difficult dinner
reservations to secure in Paris.

Dinner for one at Bouley in New York City: $90
Average cost for one person, assuming a 20% gratuity,
but not including wine. Bouley's most expensive entree is Maine lobster with mango and papaya at $36.
Its most expensive appetizer is foie gras at $21.

An airline meal: $4.55
In 1993, United Airlines spent $317 million on food
and beverages for its 69.7 million passengers—$4.55
per flyer.

Coca-Cola from room service at the $6.89
Pierre Hotel in New York City:
Actual menu price is $3.50. A cover charge ($2), a 17%
gratuity (94 cents), and 8 ¼% sales tax (45 cents) are
added on.

Average price for a cup of coffee in Kyoto, Japan: **$2.70**

Average price for a cup of coffee in   **65 cents**
Budapest, Hungary:

Bottle of very rare 50-year-old Glenfiddich   **$71,200**
Scotch whisky
This represents the world record auction price for a
bottle of whisky. Prices for rare whiskies generally
start at a few hundred dollars per bottle. In 1993, 14
bottles of Scotch whisky salvaged from a Scottish ship
that sank in 1941 were sold at auction for $1,232 apiece.

Lalique swizzle stick: **$75**
The famed French crystal company offers its "Roxane"
swizzle stick, designed by Mark Lalique and produced
in the trademark style of the company.

Bottle of Dom Pérignon Rose :   **$285**
Price as quoted by the Park Avenue Liquor Store in
New York City.

***Stupid Bar Tricks* (book):**   **$5.95**
The 95-page paperback will make you the star at your
favorite watering hole.
Source: Now That's Funny Publishing, P.O. Box 15788,
Ft. Lauderdale, FL 33318

Roast beef sandwich—

—at the Carnegie Hall Deli in NYC: **$9.45**
Served with Russian dressing on the side.

—at Arby's: **$2.99**
For a Giant Roast Beef sandwich, served with packets
of Arby's Sauce. Lettuce, tomato, and cheese extra.

1 pound of pastrami from New York's 2nd Avenue Deli: $17
"Dry cured for more than a week in salt, spices and
peppercorns, then carefully smoked to perfection . . ."
Available by mail order; can be overnight rush deliv-
ered to your location in the U.S.
Source: 2nd Avenue Deli, New York, NY (800-NYC-
DELI)

Buffalo burger at Al's Oasis in $3.15
Oacama, South Dakota:

Rattlesnake meat (per pound): $17.90
Source: D'Artagnan, 399 St. Paul Ave., Jersey City, NJ
07306 (800-DARTAGN)

Alligator tail meat (per pound): $14.65
Source: D'Artagnan, 399 St. Paul Ave., Jersey City, NJ
07306 (800-DARTAGN)

1 pound of "Rocky Mountain oysters": $2.99
Considered a delicacy by some, a gastronomic atrocity
by others, "Rocky Mountain oysters" are fresh bull tes-
ticles. If sliced and breaded, the price is $3.99 per
pound.
Source: Edwards Meats, Wheatridge, CO (303-422-
4397)

Fruit bats: $25
Fruit bats have become such a popular entree at
restaurants on Guam and other South Pacific islands
that the bat is threatened with being eaten out of existence.

Peaberry coffee from Hawaii (1 pound): $14.95
The Paradise Coffee Company roasts its coffee fresh
daily in the morning and ships it out in the afternoon.
Their finest coffee is Peaberry, "a small, dense coffee

bean which is only about 2% of the total coffee crop. This little bean comes out of the coffee fruit, which normally produces two halves of a coffee bean, which means that it is packed with flavor." Hawaii is the only U.S. state where coffee is grown.
Source: Paradise Coffee Company, P.O. Box 761, Holualoa-Kona, HI 96725 (800-347-9519)

Coffee vending machine: $2,800
Dispenses freeze-dried coffee into a paper or Styrofoam cup. A deluxe version, for $5,500, has a brew chamber that grinds the beans and serves the coffee freshly brewed.

Davidoff cigar: $19
The 8 ⅔-inch Aniversario No. 1 Tubos, hand-rolled in the Dominican Republic, is sold in packages of 10 for $190. A Davidoff cigar humidor ("The Giant," its most expensive model) holds 300 cigars, is crafted from Thuya (a rare African wood), and costs $5,640. Its best cigar scissors (gold-plated stainless steel) guarantee "the large, direct circular cut that allows the perfect amount of smoke to come through," and run $410. Davidoff's best cigar lighters cost $560. And its lead crystal ashtray, with sterling silver, goes for $1,960. All together, with a supply of 300 of the best cigars, the total bill is $14,270. Of course, even Davidoff—with stores on Madison Avenue in New York, and Rodeo Drive in Beverly Hills—has less expensive alternatives to all of these items.
Source: Davidoff of Geneva (800-328-4365)

Mushroom farm: $13.95
Small, self-contained home unit allows you to grow edible mushrooms in 30 days.
Source: Edmund Scientific Company, 101 E. Gloucester Pike, Barrington, NJ 08007 (609-573-6250)

Thanksgiving Day turkey dinner (per person):   **$2.75**
Average cost per person in the U.S. in 1993, based on a
home-cooked Thanksgiving meal for 10 people.
Source: American Farm Bureau Federation

Laboratory test for presence of   **$35**
arsenic in a food sample:
Source: Industrial Labs, P.O. Box 16207, Denver, CO
80216 (800-456-5288)

A New You

A darker, thinner, bigger, better smelling you—you can have it all. The only limits are how badly you want it and the size of your bank account. Vanity can make paupers of us all.

Treatment at a bad breath clinic: $300

The Pennsylvania Center in Philadelphia is the first dental clinic in the country to specialize in treating breath problems. Treatment normally involves three visits. If the culprit is bacteria (which it usually is), the soft tissue in the patient's mouth is scraped and then sprayed with a germicide. Patients are then instructed how to treat themselves at home using a germicide. Besides the cost of the clinic, maintaining good breath usually requires about $16 per month on a maintenance program. The clinic has proved popular since it opened in 1993—thousands have called to inquire about appointments. "The fact is," says clinic director Dr. Jon L. Richter, "for some people, bad breath is ruining their lives."
Source: Dr. Jon L. Richter, Pennsylvania Center, 4100 Walnut St., Philadelphia, PA 19104 (215-382-3776)

Tattoo, full body: $50,000

Sunset Strip Tattoo in Hollywood estimates that it would take approximately 5 years and about $50,000 (at $150 per hour) to cover an entire body with tattoos. (Another tattooist in Boise, Idaho, estimated the cost at $25,000 based on $50 per hour.) A single small tattoo may cost as little at $25. The average tattoo costs between $50 and $100.

Tattoo removal by a physician: **$2,000**
The actual cost depends on the size of the tattoo, but at $250 per square inch, a 2-inch by 4-inch tattoo would cost $2,000 to remove—several times the original cost of having it put on.

Suntanning machine: **$1,995**
The Montego Bay 16 suntanning bed is 6 ½ feet long and 2 ½ feet wide, and is advertised as a "complete home tanning center . . . for flawless tanning in just 20 minutes." The company's top-of-the-line commercial unit cuts tanning time in half, and costs $5,495.
Source: PC Marketing, Inc., 1040 Wilt Ave., Ridgefield, NJ 07657 (800-247-4301)

Suntan accelerator lotions—

—Hoss Sauce Dark (8 ounces):   **$10**
"Perfect for beginning tanners who want a good solid base."

—Hoss Sauce Super Dark (8 ounces):   **$10**
"An advanced formula to break the dreaded plateau."

—Hoss Sauce Wild Fire (9 ounces):   **$20**
"The ultimate strength maximizer for the serious tanner."
Source: PC Marketing, Inc., 1040 Wilt Ave., Ridgefield, NJ 07657 (800-247-4301)

Aesthetic plastic surgery (average surgeon's fees in the U.S.)—

—Liposuction (any single site):	**$1,622**
—Breast augmentation:	**$2,754**
—Nose reshaping (rhinoplasty):	**$2,997**
—Buttocks lift:	**$3,084**
—Tummy tuck:	**$3,618**
—Facelift:	**$4,156**

Fees are tracked by the American Society of Plastic and Reconstructive Surgeons, Inc. There can be substantial variation in the cost of a procedure from region to region. For example, facelifts average $4,026 in Florida and $5,410 in New York State. Hospital charges are extra.

Pec implants for men: $4,000
A solid silicone implant is inserted under the pectoral muscles to achieve that "pumped-up" look.

Calf implants for men: $3,000
Some calf implant procedures may run as high as $4,200.

Surgical hair transplant: $8,750
The procedure, done by a dermatologic surgeon, involves grafting plugs of hair (each containing 20 to 30 hair follicles) from the back of the head to the crown of the scalp (really a matter of rearranging what hair there is). The cost is $25 per graft. A complete transplant may take as many as 350 grafts during 3–4 sessions. The procedure works only for men who have enough hair left to be worth transplanting. The results get mixed reviews. Writer Bill Heavey has noted, "If the plugs are too obvious, your head looks like a miniature tree farm."

Rogaine "hair growth medicine" $60
(1 month's prescription):
Also known as minoxidil, Rogaine has been touted as "the only drug proven to grow hair." The drawback, according to one expert, is that "It grows hair only on some of the people some of the time."

Hair thickener: $39.92
First-time order, then $20 per reorder. The Ronco GLH Formula Number 9 Hair System is a set of 3 products:

(1) a hair cleaner; (2) a spray-on colored hair thickener that also "paints over" the bald spots; and (3) a finishing shield.
Source: Ronco (800-486-1806)

"The Works" at Elizabeth Arden in New York: $315.35
A 6 ¼-hour beauty workover that includes body massage, facial, manicure, pedicure, shampoo and haircut, makeup application—and lunch.
Source: Elizabeth Arden, 691 Fifth Ave., New York, NY (212-546-0200)

Jericho Therapeutic Dead Sea Mud (16 ounces): $29.20
Dredged from the bottom of the Salt Sea in Israel, and available at fine cosmetics counters everywhere.

Rotary nose clippers: $2.95
"Discover an easy way to remove embarrassing hair from nose and ears." Just insert the tip of the device and squeeze the handles.
Source: Puritan's Pride, P.O. Box 9001, Oakdale, NY 11769-9001 (800-645-1030)

Nose (septum) piercing: $25
Septum piercings are $25 each; nostril piercings run $20. Simple ear piercings generally cost $10 (but are free in some stores, if you buy the jewelry there), while nipple piercings are $25 each. Also pierceable are the eyebrows, lips, navel, genitals, and rectal area. Piercing jewelry includes rings, studs, loops, and bars in many shapes and sizes, available in surgical stainless steel, sterling silver, and 14K gold. Also available are decorative bones (especially popular in nose piercings). The most basic piercing jewelry can be bought for $20–$30, but more exotic items can cost over $400.
Source: Gauntlet, Inc., 2215-R Market St., Box #801, San Francisco, CA 94114 (415-252-1404)

Playing Hard

Go fishing in Alaska or golfing in Hawaii, or throw a private party for 7,000 of your closest friends. Playing hard is expensive, but bargains can be had. As you'll see, death-defying thrills are sometimes available for as little as $8 per person.

Tennis lesson with Billie Jean King: $15,000
For a 2-hour private lesson. However, King also gives free clinics for children and adults as part of the Teamtennis program.
Source: Billie Jean King, World Teamtennis, 445 N. Wells St., Suite 404, Chicago, IL 60610

A personal trainer (45-minute session): $45
Or 30 sessions for $40 each. At the Sports Training Institute, each workout is supervised one-on-one with a personal trainer. Workouts take place at STI's own facility, which was originally designed to train professional athletes. STI has facilities in New York, New Jersey, Connecticut, and California.
Source: Sports Training Institute, 239 East 49th St., New York, NY 10017 (212-752-7111)

7-day "world-class" fly fishing vacation in Alaska: $4,150

The Crystal Creek Lodge is located 320 miles southwest of Anchorage in the Bristol Bay area. Guests are flown daily, by helicopter or float-plane, to some of the best fishing spots for salmon, trout, and pike in North America. Round-trip airfare to Alaska is not included.

Source: Crystal Creek Lodge, 3819 East LaSalle, Phoenix, AZ 85040 (800-525-3153)

Greens fees at the Makena Golf Course   **$110**
at Maui, Hawaii:
Includes your choice of either of two 72-par courses. The South Course leads to the ocean, while the North Course hugs the slopes of the now-extinct volcano Haleakala. Cart rental is included.
Source: Makena Golf Course, 5415 Makena Alanui, Kihei, HI 96753 (808-879-3344)

5-day Colorado ski vacation for a family of four: **$3,040**
Average cost of $152 per skier per day includes $29 for lift tickets and ski school, $44 for lodging, $29 for meals and entertainment, and $43 for shopping. Transportation to the ski area is not included.
Source: Colorado Ski Country USA, 1560 Broadway, Suite 1440, Denver, CO 80202 (303-837-0793)

Ski lift ticket at Aspen Mountain, Colorado: **$49**
This is the daily rate from December 10 until the end of the ski season.
Source: Aspen Central Reservations Travel, 425 Rio Grande Place, Aspen, CO 81611 (800-262-7736)

Ski lift ticket at Howelsen Ski Area,   **$8**
Steamboat Springs, Colorado:
Source: Howelsen Ski Area, P.O. Box 775088, Steamboat Springs, CO 80477 (303-879-2043)

Bobsled ride at Steamboat Springs, Colorado: **$8**
Located at Howelsen Ski Area (see above). Riders barrel down a 4,200-foot course between glistening walls of ice at speeds up to 50 mph. There are only two other public bobsled courses in the U.S.: one at Vail, Colorado, and the other at Lake Placid, New York.

Complete scuba diving gear: $1,200

Includes two tanks, wet suit, BC jacket, regulator with
alternate air source, and console with compass and
gauges for pressure, depth, etc. Prices for some scuba
gear can run considerably higher. For example, an in-
tergrated computer that attaches to the gear can cost
$800 extra. Scuba diving lessons can usually be had for
about $165 for group instruction, $350 for private
lessons.
Source: Miami Aqualung, Miami, FL (305-225-3483)

Complete set of (12) Life Circuit exercise machines: $86,400

The computerized strength-training system consists of
12 separate machines ($7,200 each) that exercise every
major part of the body. Quantity discounts are available, but only for those buying multiple sets of the machines.
Source: Life Fitness, 10601 West Belmont Ave.,
Franklin Park, IL 60131 (800-351-3737)

Life Step 9500 HR stair machine: $2,995

This commercial stair machine has a new feature not
found in most aerobic exercisers—with one's hands on
the support bar, it monitors pulse and adjusts machine
speed to maintain a target pulse rate.
Source: Life Fitness, 10601 West Belmont Ave.,
Franklin Park, IL 60131 (800-351-3737)

Adler Monarch pool table: $15,750

The 9-foot by 4 ½-foot Monarch is Adler's most expensive model. Made of solid walnut (and designed to re-
semble pool tables from the mid-19th century), it
features massive legs carved into the shape of crouch-
ing lions. Rosewood, oak, ebony, holly, laurel, and
tulipwood are used in the rails, panels, and inlays. In
contrast, Adler's ultra-modern Atlantis pool table
($11,950) has no legs, but uses a shimmering, stainless-
steel, inverted pyramid for support. Adler's handcrafted, custom-built models start at $3,250.
Source: Pool Tables by Adler, 10100 Aviation Blvd., Los
Angeles, CA 90045 (213-410-9873)

El Toro mechanical bull: $7,500
Featured at Gilley's Club ("The World's Largest Night Club") in Pasadena, Texas, where it can be ridden for a fraction of the purchase price. John Travolta and Debra Winger made them famous in the movie *Urban Cowboy*.
Source: Art's Music & Cigarette Service, 2428 Sam Houston Parkway, Pasadena, TX 77503 (713-998-9544)

Electric golf cart: $3,500
Price is for a basic golf cart without extras. A high-end deluxe model—retailing for about $10,000—includes 24K gold-plated spokes, 5-inch color TV, head and tail and brake lights, AM/FM radio, horn, and plush carpeting. A fully enclosed cab with a fiberglass body can cost up to $15,000.
Source: Columbia Par Car—The Masters, Colorado Springs, CO (800-253-3883)

Backyard golf driving range: $2,895
Includes steel tubing framework and heavy-duty golf mesh netting. Options such as automatic ball return and teeing device, distance monitor (the golf ball's "distance" is posted on a scoreboard), and coin-op ball dispenser can drive the price up to $13,750. Commercial multi-station units are also available.
Source: Creative Athletic Products and Service, Inc., Box 7731, Des Moines, IA 50322 (800-227-4574)

20- by 40-foot swimming pool (average cost): $17,000
The National Spa and Pool Institute estimates that the average 20-foot by 40-foot in-ground residential pool (in concrete) costs from $17,000 to $25,000. The same size pool with a vinyl lining is $12,000 to $16,000. Price does not include heater, decking, or diving board. There are approximately 3.3 million in-ground residential pools in the U.S. Families that own them have an average income of $66,000.

•   •   •

Removable "dome" for an outdoor   **$35,200**
swimming pool:
For a 15-foot-high structure (30 feet wide and 30 feet
long) with aluminum frame and vinyl-coated polyester
covering, designed to be put up in winter and taken
down in the summer. Includes heating, ventilation,
lighting, and complete installation. Larger pools are
more expensive to enclose. An 18- by 50- by 80-foot
"dome" costs $105,000. Similar enclosures are also
available for tennis courts: a 30- by 60- by 120-foot
structure costs $145,400.
Source: Sport Span Systems, Inc., P.O. Box 995, Blue
Bell, PA 19422 (215-654-1941)

Portable tennis ball machine: **$1,195**
Hopper holds up to 250 balls. Remote control is $300
extra. For baseball practice, a Curveball Pitching Machine is available for $1,555, and a Softball Pitching
Machine for $995. (Both throw at speeds of up to 70
mph.) A Soccer Machine ($1,495) accurately serves a
soccer ball at various speeds and spins. A Football Machine ($1,655) "throws perfect punts, kickoffs, or
passes to any precise spot on your field."
Source: The JUGS Co., P.O. Drawer 365, Tualatin, OR
97062 (800-547-6843)

Snow-making machine: **$1,200**
Overnight, the Z-1 Snowgun will cover 2–3 acres with
1 foot of artificial snow. The colder the temperature,
the more snow the machine is capable of making. It
takes about 50,000 gallons of water to cover an acre
with 1 foot of snow. Or put another way, 1 inch of water makes 4–8 inches of artificial snow. Some large ski
areas use as many as 200–300 snow-making machines
to keep the slopes covered.
Source: Larchmont Engineering, Chelmsford, MA
(508-250-1260)

Leasing the Houston Astrodome for a day: **$25,000**
Basic cost to rent the facility with lights and air-condi-
tioning. All other expenses of operating the stadium—

such as staffing, stage sound and stage lighting, and cleanup—are extra. The total cost of renting the Astrodome for a concert, for example, could easily exceed $200,000.
Source: Houston Astrodome, Houston, TX (713-799-9631)

Renting Disneyland for a private party: **$133,000**
The park charges $19 per person, but insists on a minimum of 7,000 people.
Source: Disneyland, Anaheim, CA (714-502-3900)

The Sporting Life

You may not be able to play with the pros, but it's possible to surround yourself with all the trappings of professional sports. A genuine major-league baseball isn't that expensive, but a set of NFL-style goal posts will set you back several months' salary.

Baseball uniform for a major-league player: $255
Caps cost $15 to $20, jerseys $75 to $100, pants $60 to $65, and cleats about $75. A batter's helmet runs an additional $30 to $35.
Source: Rawlings Sporting Goods, St. Louis, MO

Professional football player's uniform: $675
The jersey and pants cost $100, shoulder pads $200 to $250, girdle with hip, thigh, and buttocks pads $50, knee pads $25, cleats $100, and helmet about $200.
Source: Rawlings Sporting Goods, St. Louis, MO

Professional basketball player's uniform: $400
The warm-up uniform is $150, the game uniform (shorts and top) $100, and the shoes about $150.
Source: Rawlings Sporting Goods, St. Louis, MO

Professional hockey player's uniform: $983
The jersey costs $160, pants and suspenders $95, shoulder pads $135, elbow pads $70, shin pads $125, garter belt $3, protective cup $40, helmet $75, and skates $280.

Pro-style football: $80
Source: Rawlings Sporting Goods, St. Louis, MO

Major-league baseball bat: $25
By comparison, aluminum bats (which are popular outside the professional ranks) cost about $75 each, but are less expensive in the long run since they don't break.
Source: Rawlings Sporting Goods, St. Louis, MO

Pro-style baseball: $10
Source: Rawlings Sporting Goods, St. Louis, MO

Baseball glove (professional): $160
Rawlings Sporting Goods makes about 80 different models for professional players. Prices range from $160 to $200. Each glove is designed according to the special requirements of the various field positions. Players and their teams don't have to worry about the high price: they usually get the gloves free in exchange for promotional considerations. Brown and black are the most popular colors, but blue is also available.
Source: Rawlings Sporting Goods, St. Louis, MO

Pro-style hockey stick: $27
(Galvanized rubber pucks cost $60 for 100.)

NFL-style goal posts (set of 2): $5,000
The upright posts are 23 feet 4 inches apart, and the horizontal post is 10 feet off the ground.
Source: Austin Athletic Equipment Corp., Bellmore, NY (516-785-0100)

Pro-style basketball: $85
Source: Rawlings Sporting Goods, St. Louis, MO

NBA-style backboard: **$700**
The backboards are made of glass, and measure 4 feet
by 6 feet. An entire pro-style hoop can cost up to $5,000,
including the pole, backboard, and breakaway rim.
Source: Austin Athletic Equipment Corp., Bellmore,
NY (516-785-0100)

Olympic-style hurdle: **$134.95**
The 30-pound UCS Olympic Hurdle (official hurdle of
the '84, '88, and '92 Olympic Games) adjusts to a
height of 42 inches.
Source: M-F Athletic Co., P.O. Box 8090, Cranston, RI
02920 (800-556-7464)

Relay baton (aluminum):   **$2.20**
Available in six colors.
Source: M-F Athletic Co., P.O. Box 8090, Cranston, RI
02920 (800-556-7464)

Men's 800-gram javelin: **$599**
The Nemeth Men's 90+ is designed for ranges over 90
meters. A women's 400-gram javelin can be bought for
as little as $85. Carrying tubes are about $200 extra.
Source: M-F Athletic Co., P.O. Box 8090, Cranston, RI
02920 (800-556-7464)

Vaulting pole (16 ½ feet):   **$392**
The top-of-the-line, high-performance Pacer carbon
fiber pole has a test weight of 200 pounds. High-performance poles have fast bending and unbending ac-
tion, and are designed for vaulters clearing 12 feet and
higher. At the low end of the price range, a 10-foot 9-
inch training pole (with a test weight of 70 to 90
pounds) costs about $79.
Source: M-F Athletic Co., P.O. Box 8090, Cranston, RI
02920 (800-556-7464)

• • •

Discus (2 kilograms): $229.95

The Cantabrian Hyper-Spin, with a solid aluminum bronze alloy rim, has 85% of its weight distributed to the outside rim. A rubber training model discus can be had for $11.50.

Source: M-F Athletic Co., P.O. Box 8090, Cranston, RI 02920 (800-556-7464)

Shot put (16 pounds): $149.95

A competition-class steel shot is 129 millimeters in diameter, and has been machined to attain as perfect roundness as possible. A lightweight iron shot, weighing only 5 pounds, can be bought for $7.95.

Source: M-F Athletic Co., P.O. Box 8090, Cranston, RI 02920 (800-556-7464)

Parallel bars: $3,400

Super Elite parallel bars are constructed with chrome-plated pistons, and adjust to heights of 53 ½ to 78 ¾ inches and widths of 15 ⅓ to 26 ⅓ inches. They meet all specifications of the Federation of International Gymnastics.

Source: Gerstung Manufacturing and Sales, 6308-10 Blair Hill Lane, Baltimore, MD 21209 (410-337-7781)

Pommel horse: $2,600

Heavy-duty Elite pommel horse meets all Federation of International Gymnastics specifications.

Source: Gerstung Manufacturing and Sales, 6308-10 Blair Hill Lane, Baltimore, MD 21209 (410-337-7781)

Pair of boxing gloves (professional): $112

Everlast Model 2110-6 10-ounce heavyweight gloves, the type used by Evander Holyfield. Boxing gloves are usually sold as a set of two pairs, since each boxer in a match must use identical gloves.

Source: Everlast Sporting Goods Mfg. Co., Inc., 750 East 132nd St., Bronx, NY 10454 (718-993-0100)

Badminton shuttlecock (birdie): $2.30

Regulation tournament-play badminton birdie is made of 16 goose feathers from the identical wings of 4 different geese. The feathers are inserted into a goatskin-covered cork. Because these birdies tend to lose their feathers, they last for only one or two games. Sold by the dozen for $27.60.

Source: Esses Distributing Co., 1627 Washington Ave., St. Louis, MO 63103 (314-231-9434)

Bleachers (seats 50): $1,163

15 feet long with 5 rows. Has 10-inch-wide aluminum seats with galvanized steel framework. Available in various sizes.
Source: M-F Athletic Co., P.O. Box 8090, Cranston, RI 02920 (800-556-7464)

Olympic gold medal: $364

Although each Games' medals may vary in their surface design, depending on the wishes of the host city, the International Olympic Committee has certain regulations regarding their size and composition. Each medal must be at least 60 millimeters (2 ¼ inches) in diameter and 3 millimeters (⅛ inch) thick. The first- and second-place medals must be made of silver that is at least 92.5% pure. In addition, first-place medals must be heavily gilded with at least 6 grams of gold. All medals must come attached to some sort of chain or ribbon, to be hung around the necks of the winning athletes. Jostens Canada Ltd. manufactured the medals for the 1988 Olympic Winter Games at Calgary. The company valued the gold medals at $364, silver at $144, and bronze at $55. Winners aren't the only recipients of medals. Almost everyone involved in the Calgary Games—all athletes, coaches, officials, and dignitaries (some 36,725 people in all)—received some kind of commemorative medal. What's more, medals aren't the only thing that winners receive. The U.S. Olympic Committee also pays cash awards to its athletes: $15,000 to gold medalists, $10,000 to silver medalists, and $7,500 to bronze medalists.

Olympic-style figure skates: $750

The custom-made boots cost about $500 and the blades are an additional $250–$450.

Source: Harlick, 893 America St., San Carlos, CA 94070 (415-593-2093)

Spectator Sports

The most renowned and impressive sporting events in the world are yours to experience firsthand—from the Kentucky Derby to a Chicago Bulls game—all for the price of a ticket. Just be prepared to pay hard.

Courtside seat at a Chicago Bulls game: $300

There are only about 100 courtside seats available. A courtside seat for the entire year would cost $13,200. Other seats in the 17,339-seat Chicago Stadium cost from $19 to $110, with playoff and championship games bringing slightly higher prices (from $22 to $325). However, every Chicago Bulls game has been sold out since the 1987 season, and at last count there was a waiting list of 11,000 for season tickets.
Source: Chicago Bulls, One Magnificent Mile, 980 North Michigan Ave., Suite 1600, Chicago, IL 60611 (312-943-5800)

Renting a private suite at the Houston Astrodome for Houston Oilers' games (whole season): $65,000

The suite has 36 seats. Food and beverage service are not included in the price. Another suite, with only 18 seats, can be rented for $45,000 per season. By comparison, regular seating costs $18 to $45 per game.
Source: Houston Oilers, 6910 Fannin St., Lower Level, Houston, TX 77030 (713-797-9111)

• • •

Tickets to the Super Bowl: $175
Other than a few tickets for suite seating, all tickets are
$175. The National Football League conducts a lottery
each year in an attempt to distribute tickets more
fairly.
Source: National Football League, 410 Park Ave.,
New York, NY 10022 (212-758-1500)

Seat at the U.S. Open Tennis Tournament (finals): $55
The tournament is held annually in late August and
early September at Flushing Meadows in Queens,
New York. Seating is on a first-come, first-serve basis.
Semifinal and final rounds are $55, quarterfinals $36.
Seating for early round play starts at $18.
Source: U.S. Tennis Association, 1212 Avenue of the
Americas, New York, NY 10036 (212-302-3322)

Ticket to the INDY 500: $25
The majority of tickets are in the $55–$65 range, with
some (for upper-level seating in the penthouse) going
for as high as $110. Like most major national sporting
events, tickets sell out nearly a year in advance.
Source: Indianapolis Motor Speedway, P.O. Box 24152,
Speedway, IN 46224 (317-248-6750)

Tickets to the World Series (per game): $45
$60 for the best seats. The average ticket price for a
regular-season Major League Baseball game in 1994
was $10.45, and the total cost for a family of 4 to attend
a game was $95.80, according to a survey by Team
Marketing Report.
Source: Baseball Commissioner's Office, 350 Park Ave.,
New York, NY 10022 (212-371-7800)

Ringside seat at a World Heavyweight Boxing Match: $1,000
$500–$1,200 was the going rate for the best seats in the
house when Evander Holyfield fought and defeated
Riddick Bowe in Las Vegas on November 6, 1993.

Ticket to the Kentucky Derby: **$20**

This is the price for grandstand and infield seats. Seats in the clubhouse are $10 higher. At other times, admission to Churchill Downs costs $2 (grandstands) and $3.50 (clubhouse).

Source: Churchill Downs, 700 Central Ave., Louisville, KY 40208 (502-636-4400)

Ticket to the Masters Golf Tournament: **$100**

The ticket is good for 4 days of championship play at the tournament, which is held each April at the Augusta National Golf Club in Augusta, Georgia. The U.S. Open, which is held at a different course each year in June, is more expensive—$200 for the event, or $50 per day. Admission to practice days at either tournament costs the same: $15–$25.

Source: Augusta National Golf Club, P.O. Box 2086, Augusta, GA 30913; (706-738-7761)

Ticket to the Lobster Race & Oyster Fest   **$4**
at Aiken, South Carolina:

$4 in advance, $5 at the door. Billed as "the world's only thoroughbred lobster races," the races are held the first Saturday in May, the same time as the Kentucky Derby. The actual "track" that the lobsters race in (called "Lobster Downs") is filled with salt water.

Source: Aiken, South Carolina, Chamber of Commerce (800-641-1111)

Natural Wonders

Whether it came from outer space or the bottom of the sea or from the pre-historic past, it's all available now, thanks to some enterprising merchants. It may have been handcrafted by nature but it's being sold retail.

Complete frog or lizard preserved intact in amber: **$40,000**
An intact scorpion costs about $20,000. Amber-encrusted leaves or insects (such as gnats and ants) may cost anywhere from $12 to $300. Interest in these prehistoric specimens soared after the release of the film *Jurassic Park* in 1993.

Dinosaur (triceratops) skeleton: **$1.225 million**
A museum-quality triceratops skull can be had for $185,000. Also available: dinosaur footprints ($400–$1,800), and a 26-million-year-old saber-toothed tiger skull ($12,000), "an excellent investment that will appreciate in value."
Source: The Dinosaur Store, 26664 Seagull Way, Suite B-117, Malibu, CA 90265 (310-589-5988)

A dinosaur egg: **$7,130**
Ten sauropod eggs, laid more than 70 million years ago, were sold at Bonham's auction house in London in 1993 for $71,300 for the lot.

Fish fossil (4–6 inches): $30

An "extra-fine" fossil of a Miocene fish (4 to 6 inches),
from the Green River Formation, Wyoming.
Source: Bitner's, P.O. Box 9367, Phoenix, AZ 85068
(800-BITNERS)

Replica of a 10,600-year-old mammoth: $25,000

Fiberglass replicas of mammoth skeletons are made by
the Prehistoric Museum at the College of Eastern
Utah. The mammoth from which the replicas are made
is the most complete and best-preserved specimen
ever located. Each replica takes about 4 weeks to complete, stands 14 feet high, and can be fashioned in any
pose you desire.
Source: Prehistoric Museum, College of Eastern Utah,
400 E. 4th North, Price, UT 84501 (801-637-5060)

An iron meteorite: $1,000

8-pound meteorite, excavated from Sikhote-Alin in the
former Soviet Union. Prices for meteorites vary widely
depending on the type, the location where they are
found, and any unusual or distinguishing surface features. Tiny ones can be had for as little as $10. More
impressive and unusual specimens can go for more
than $10,000.
Source: Robert A. Haag ("The Meteorite Man"), P.O.
Box 27527, Tucson, AZ 85726

Venus flytrap plant: $5.75

Peter Pauls Nurseries in Canandaigua, New York, carries a complete line of carnivorous plants.
Source: Peter Pauls Nurseries, Canandaigua, NY 14424
(716-394-7397)

Saguaro cactus (with arms): $400

The value of a plant is determined not so much by size
as by shape. ("It's a beauty contest," explains one
dealer.) A saguaro with no arms might bring only
$20–$40, while larger specimens with interesting arms
can cost well over $1,000. Saguaros are regulated and

protected in Arizona: it is illegal to dig one up in the desert, and moving one requires a permit from the Arizona Department of Agriculture.
Source: Arizona Cactus Sales, 1619 South Arizona, Chandler, AZ 85248 (602-963-1061)

Rare *Paphiopedilum* (lady slipper) orchid: $3,000
A rare variety of lady slipper orchids 12 to 18 inches high in 3- to 4-inch pots can cost from $1,000 to $3,000. They're the most expensive species of plant sold by Rod McClellan Orchids of South San Francisco. Some of the company's one-of-a-kind breeding plants also cost up to several thousand dollars.
Source: Rod McClellan Orchids, 1450 El Camino Real, S. San Francisco, CA 94080 (415-871-5655)

Admission to the Cecil B. Day Butterfly Center at Callaway Gardens in Georgia: $7.50
The center includes a 2,500-acre horticultural display as well as an 8,000-square-foot, octagon-shaped, glass-enclosed tropical butterfly conservatory, home to more than 1,000 butterflies—the largest display of living butterflies in North America.
Source: Callaway Gardens Resort, Inc., Pine Mountain, GA 31822-2000 (404-663-5187)

Human brain: $284
Intact human brain embalmed in odorless fluid and suitable for dissection or display. Suppliers will generally sell brains only to schools and other institutions for educational and research purposes.
Source: Carolina Biological Supply Company, 2700 York Road, Burlington, NC 27215-3393 (800-334-5551)

Human skeleton: $1,300
Complete and authentic natural bone skeleton comes unassembled (or "disarticulated") and has some minor, inevitable stains and imperfections. Wooden carrying

case is $110 extra. An assembled life-size plastic human skeleton sells for about $430.

Source: Carolina Biological Supply Company, 2700 York Road, Burlington, NC 27215-3393 (800-334-5551)

Giant ant farm: $19.95

Plastic see-through case allows you to watch the ants at work. Farms do not come with the ants inside, but include a certificate redeemable to have the ants shipped to you after purchase of the farm. (Ants cannot be shipped to Tennessee or Hawaii.)

Source: Edmund Scientific Company, 101 E. Gloucester Pike, Barrington, NJ 08007 (609-573-6250)

An electron microscope: $65,000

Scanning electron microscopes (SEMs) range in price from $65,000 to $300,000. An electron beam scans the sample surface to give a view of the surface topography. Conventional optical microscopes lose depth of focus at 20,000X to 30,000X magnification, whereas an SEM has excellent depth of focus up to 500,000X. Such power enables biologists, for example, to identify a plant species merely by looking at individual pollen grains. A transmission electron microscope (TEM) transmits an electron beam *through* the sample to magnetic lenses that project the image on a screen. TEMs can magnify to 1,000,000X—giving scientists views of molecules or even individual atoms. TEMs cost from $150,000 to as much as $4 million.

Source: Carl Zeiss, 1 Zeiss Drive, Thornwood, NY 10594 (914-747-1800)

Earthquake recorder: $6,950

Basic, above-ground system for recording and measuring earthquakes consists of an SS-1 Ranger Seismometer connected to a VR-2 Drum Recorder. Highly sensitive and sophisticated seismographs, such as those used at nuclear power plants, can cost $100,000 and more.

Source: Kinemetrics, Inc., 222 Vista Ave., Pasadena, CA 91107 (818-897-2220)

"Penises of the Animal Kingdom,"   **$8.95**
comparative anatomy chart:
A 23-inch by 35-inch chart depicts the male copulatory
organs of several animals, from man to whale.
Source: Scientific Novelty Co., P.O. Box 673-D, Bloom-
ington, IN 47402

Not So Cheap Thrills

Why stand in line to ride the roller coaster or see the latest hit movie? What's the point of paying the "house" a commission to play its slot machines? Own your own theme park, your own movie theater, your own casino. Just remember, cheap thrills they aren't.

65 ⅓-foot Ferris wheel: $400,000

Portable model, capable of being transported from carnival to carnival. A 90-foot-diameter portable model costs about $875,000.
Source: Chance Rides, P.O. Box 12328, Wichita, KS 67277 (316-942-7411)

Roller coaster: $8 million

$8 million to $12 million is the price range for a complete, installed, state-of-the-art theme park roller coaster, such as the 80-mph Steel Phantom (the world's fastest) at Kennywood Park, Pennsylvania, or the 205-foot-high Magnum XL-200 (the world's tallest) at Cedar Point Park in Sandusky, Ohio. A much tamer, 18-passenger motor-driven roller coaster for children (made by Zamperla) costs $180,000.
Source: Arrow Dynamics, Clearfield, UT (801-825-1611)

Bumper car ride: $426,000

Portable ride (trailer included). Consists of 24 bumper cars (powered by DC electricity) in a 90-foot-long, 2,700-square-foot building illuminated by 5,000 lights.

A 12-car, 1,400-square-foot portable setup costs $185,000. Non-portable models are less expensive. A single bumper car costs $4,000–$5,000.
Source: Majestic Manufacturing Co., 4536 St. Rt. #7, New Waterford, OH 44445 (216-457-2447)

50-foot Grand carousel: $350,000

Large carousels cost from $350,000 to $1 million. Installation adds as much as $100,000. Prices vary according to the kind of flooring (tread plate or oak), the type of mirrors used (regular or antique beveled glass), and whether the carousel is hand-painted. The animals (there are 60 animals, as well as 2 chariots, on the Grand model) cost from $2,200 apiece to $7,000 for highly detailed animals modeled after turn-of-the-century designs.
Source: Chance Rides, P.O. Box 12328, Wichita, KS 67277 (316-942-7411)

Antique wood carousel horse: $2,500

52-inch-long "jumper" horse is freshly restored but comparatively plain. Carousel Corner in Clarkston, Michigan, has painted ponies up to $23,000, for a flashy "stander," circa 1910. In 1989, Sotheby's sold a rare carousel rooster for $148,000.
Source: Carousel Corner, Box 420, Clarkston, MI 48347 (313-625-1233)

70-millimeter commercial movie projector: $58,000

Complete system includes projector, lenses, lamphouse, platter, sound system, and automation. The projector alone (without lenses) costs $25,000.
Source: Claco Equipment and Service, Salt Lake City, UT (801-355-1250)

Movie theater projection screen (14 by 32 feet): $1,039

Movie screens are custom-made, and are sold by the square foot. (Installation is extra.) A matte white surface is the cheapest, and costs $2.32 per square foot. A more

expensive, pearlescent surface gives a sharper film image, and is $4.39 per square foot.
Source: Claco Equipment and Service, Salt Lake City, UT (801-355-1250)

22-minute traditional fireworks display: **$17,000**
Fireworks by Grucci (the firm responsible for fireworks displays at the last four presidential inaugurations, as well as for the 1986 Statue of Liberty centennial celebration) charges from $4,000 for a manually fired 8-minute traditional display to $25,000 for a 26-minute program. More sophisticated, state-of-the-art displays (featuring a choreography of fireworks and music) can cost from $30,000 for 18 minutes to $100,000 for a 30-minute "world-class" show. The Statue of Liberty display (the largest ever) cost $1.7 million. It consisted of eleven $100,000 programs fired from 11 separate sites (plus $600,000 in miscellaneous expenses). A single fireworks shell costs from $16 to $115 (a 3-burst, red, white, and blue shell is $45).
Source: Fireworks by Grucci, Inc., One Grucci Lane, Brookhaven, NY 11719 (516-286-0088)

Casino roulette wheel with layout: **$9,857**
Source: Langworthy Casino Supply, Inc., Las Vegas, NV (702-382-6285)

Casino craps table: **$4,939**
Source: Langworthy Casino Supply, Inc., Las Vegas, NV (702-382-6285)

Bally slot machine: **$4,795**
Source: Bally Gaming, Inc., Las Vegas, NV (702-896-7777)

Bally video poker machine: **$4,595**
Source: Bally Gaming, Inc., Las Vegas, NV (702-896-7777)

• • •

Pinball machine—"Tommy Pinball Wizard": $3,000

This is the going price for most state-of-the-art pinball machines. A "Star Trek: The Next Generation" pinball machine costs $3,400. Used but reconditioned machines start at about $300.

CD jukebox: $4,300

The Rowe CD51 holds 51 compact discs. 100-disc models cost $4,895. A CD-equipped replica of an old-style Wurlitzer jukebox costs $7,500.

Complete bowling lane with automatic pinsetter: $40,000

Approximate cost, installed, for a single Brunswick bowling lane. Includes ball return, gutters, masking unit, and automatic pinsetter (which by itself costs $15,000).
Source: Brunswick Corp., Muskegon, MI (616-725-3300)

Set of 10 bowling pins: $130

Source: Brunswick Corp., Muskegon, MI (616-725-3300)

A performance by Phyllis Diller: $50,000

For her standard comedy act. Does not include expenses.
Source: Phyllis Diller, 163 S. Rockingham Ave., Los Angeles, CA 90049

Hiring a three-ring circus for a performance: $70,000

For a 2-hour show by Circus Larsson under the Big Top, with seating for 3,000–4,000. Does not include traveling expenses. Circus Larsson features clowns, big cats, high-wire and trapeze acts, magicians, jugglers, elephants, a circus band, and more. Specific circus themes (such as "Alice in Wonderland") are available. A small show, depending on the location and the time of year, can be had for as little as $20,000.
Source: Circus Larsson, P.O. Box 1632, N. Miami, FL 33261 (305-895-1333)

A speech by talk show host Larry King: **$50,000**
Source: *The Larry King Show,* Mutual Broadcasting System, 1755 South Jefferson Davis Highway, Arlington, VA 22202

A cameo appearance on *Murphy Brown*:   **$4,000**
Sold to the highest bidder at a 1992 charity auction.

Hiring the "Clinton family" for 1 day: **$1,500**
Or $700 for 1 hour. Michael Newell ("Bill Clinton"), Kate Vess ("Hillary"), and young Jessica Sylman ("Chelsea") work together as "The Clinton Clones" or separately for a reduced rate. Newell, winner of the *National Enquirer*'s Bill Clinton look-alike contest, says he always wears a bullet-proof vest when performing as the president: "The kind of person who would go out and kill the president would not have the forethought to . . . make sure he has the right guy."
Source: Michael Newell, P.O. Box 621091, Littleton, CO 80162-1091 (303-797-2635)

Hiring a Madonna look-alike: **$750**
For a limited appearance, 1 to 2 hours. The Gina Lennon "look-alike" agency, Illusions, can book 4,000 look-alikes worldwide. Besides Madonna, Illusions' roster includes "Charlie Chaplin," "Barbara Bush," "Truman Capote," "Andy Warhol," and even "Rudolph Giuliani." Prices vary according to the celebrity, the nature of the event, and the length of the appearance, and travel is almost always extra, but $300–$3,000 covers the cost of employing most celebrity imposters.
Source: Illusions, 315 West Sunrise Highway, Freeport, NY 11520 (516-546-3554)

Singing telegram delivered by a stripper: **$145**
You can choose a "Chubby-Gram" (delivered by an overweight performer), or a "Shock-a-Gram" (delivered by a female impersonator). They will sing and strip for 15 to 20 minutes, but that's *all* they do.
Source: Stripper Elite, Las Vegas, NV (702-477-7719)

The Doctor's Bill

Whoever coined the phrase "being taken for a ride" might have been think-ing of ambulance service. But when it comes to the cost of medical ser-vices, getting to the hospital is just the start. Pity there's no cure for debtum medicus.

30-day treatment program for alcohol and   **$12,000**
drug dependency at the Betty Ford Center:
The famed 80-bed center is located at the Eisenhower
Medical Center near Palm Springs, California.
Source: Betty Ford Center at Eisenhower, 39000 Bob
Hope Drive, Rancho Mirage, CA 92270 (619-773-4100)

"Psychic" surgery in Santa Fe, New Mexico   **$85**
(per session):
Psychic surgeon Joanna Corti performs 11 to 15 psychic
surgeries per week while in a trancelike state. She
functions as a medium for "spirit psychic surgeons"
who work on the patient "much the same way as a
team of doctors would work on a patient in a regular
hospital operating theater." About half of her business
is done over the phone, and each session takes about
an hour. Among the diverse ailments she treats are de-pression, cysts, polyps, fertility problems, sciatica, and
headaches.
Source: Joanna Corti, Santa Fe, NM (505-989-1460)

• • •

Prenatal video of your child: **$75**
A Womb's Eyeview of Los Angeles will make a 30-minute video—actually a sonogram, which creates an image by bouncing high-frequency sound waves off the uterus—of your unborn child. Companies are forming around the country to meet the demands of expectant parents to view their offspring *in utero*. They generally charge from $75 to $150 for these "prenatal portraits."
Source: Womb's Eyeview, Los Angeles, CA (213-295-BABY)

13-day stay at the Pritikin Longevity Center: **$6,555**
The center, with facilities in Santa Monica and Miami Beach, offers a resident lifestyle-enhancement program: "the 3-in-1 Pritikin Approach of eating the right foods, maintaining a practical exercise plan, and effectively managing your stress—the keys to a lifestyle of renewed energy and vitality." More than 60,000 people have participated in the centers' programs. Studies document the program's benefits in controlling high blood pressure, diabetes, angina, high cholesterol, obesity, smoking, and gout. According to one study, 80% of program participants previously recommended for bypass surgery still had not required that surgery 5 years later. For people with more demanding health problems, a 26-day program is available for $11,181. Prices include accommodations, medical evaluation, all meals, lifestyle counseling, cooking workshops, fitness training, and entertainment. Charges for a companion are $2,831 (13-day) and $5,373 (26-day).
Source: Pritikin Longevity Center, 1910 Ocean Front Walk, Santa Monica, CA 90405 (800-421-9911)

Organ transplants (first-year cost)—
—Heart transplant: **$209,100**
—Lung transplant: **$243,600**
—Kidney transplant: **$87,700**
Charges are for patient evaluation and pre-transplant care, organ procurement, and hospital and physician fees. The current waiting list (for all organs) is over

30,000. Due to a shortage of donors, some experts believe that compensation should be paid to the families of the donors—such payments are currently illegal.
Source: The Transplant Foundation, Richmond, VA (804-285-5115)

Artificial nose or ear: $2,500
Handcrafted and custom-fitted, they are held in place with medical adhesive.

Complete set of dentures: $1,500
Average cost in the United States for a complete set of upper and lower dentures provided by a dentist who is a general practitioner; specialists may charge considerably more. Includes routine post-delivery care.

Artificial eye: $3,500
Includes eyelid, eyelashes, eyebrow, and surrounding tissue (complete orbital prosthesis). Artificial eyes, incidentally, are made of plastic not glass.
Source: American Optical Corp., Southbridge, MA (508-765-2169)

Artificial (prosthetic) arm: $5,000
The patient's cost for a complete "above-the-elbow" prosthetic arm. A below-the-elbow prosthesis is about $3,000, including an artificial hand. An electrically powered artificial arm (called a myoelectric prosthesis) costs about $8,000–$9,000 for below-the-elbow and $35,000–$40,000 for above-the-elbow.

Wheelchair: $450
Emerson-Jennings wheelchairs start at about $450 but can cost as much as $4,000 for models with wider frames, better seats, and stainless-steel frames. Sports models (for athletic competition) have lighter weight frames than standard wheelchairs, as well as tapered wheels for quick motion and quick-release axles; they're priced from $1,600 to $3,100.

Electric wheelchair: $3,400
Base price. Customized models can cost up to $20,000.
For example, a "sip & puff" feature allows a paralyzed
user to control wheelchair movement by various
modes of inhalation and exhalation. A stair-climbing
wheelchair, controlled by 8 onboard computers, costs
$27,500.

A 1-year prescription for Prozac (20 milligrams): $761.28
1 capsule per day, at $2.09 each. Reporting on the re-
cent surging sales of Prozac and other antidepressants,
the trade magazine *American Druggist* commented,
"Indeed, the depression category has no need to sing
the blues." Given that the retail cost of pharmaceuticals
is increasing at about three times the rate of inflation,
the price listed here has probably changed.

1 tablet of Marinol (5 milligrams): $5.78
Marinol is a synthetic form of the active ingredient in
marijuana, THC, and is primarily prescribed to people
with glaucoma or suffering nausea as a result of cancer
treatment or AIDS.

Bottle of milk of magnesia at a Florida hospital: $33.64
As reported in 1992.

Bottle of milk of magnesia at Kmart: $4.57
For a 12-ounce bottle.

**1-month supply of blood pressure
medication (90 tablets)—**

—Inderal (40 milligrams): $19.32

—The generic form of Inderal (40 milligrams): $6.63

1-year supply of oxygen (if used 24 hours a day): $3,819
Oxygen costs about 10 cents per cubic foot. A person
breathing pure oxygen uses about 4.5 cubic feet per

hour. Rental of the oxygen apparatus (large tank) is about $50 per month extra.

Pint of blood: $80

Hospital's cost for blood used in transfusions. Patient pays an extra $56 for testing to determine donor/recipient compatibility, and an extra $112 for administration of the transfusion.

Average hospital charges in the Denver area for—

—Coronary bypass surgery: $53,536

—Major joint and limb reattachment (lower extremity): $21,299

—Appendectomy: $6,142

—Vaginal delivery (without complications): $3,311

Charges compiled by the Colorado Hospital Association. Does not include doctors' fees. The average hospital bill in Colorado in 1993 was $10,310 (for an average stay of 4.9 days); however, the average amount actually *collected* by the hospital was only $6,540.

***In vitro* fertilization of a human embryo (per cycle):** $7,000

In vitro fertilization costs $7,000—$8,000 per cycle. On average, two to three cycles are needed to achieve fertilization. The process begins with an initial investigation to determine the causes of infertility. This costs about $1,200 without surgery, apart from the cost of the fertilization cycles. The *in vitro* fertilization procedure includes office visits, sonograms, retrieval of eggs, sperm collection, and embryo transplantation into the uterus. It also includes the use of drugs such as pergonol to stimulate ovulation. More than 15,000 babies have been born through this procedure since 1981.

Ambulance ride in New Orleans: $175

Base price for BLS (basic life support) service. ALS (advanced life support, for life-and-death situations) costs

$320. There's also a $7 per mile charge for both types of service. Medical services and supplies are also extra. For example, starting an IV costs $38, while an EKG monitor is $50.

Helicopter ambulance service (average cost per flight): **$5,000**

Ambulance (van type), fully equipped: **$77,000**
Source: Collins Ambulance Corp., Hutchinson, KS (316-663-4441)

X-ray technician's lead-lined apron: **$46.50**
An apron with thicker lead runs $65.95.
Source: Henry Schein, Inc., 5 Harbor Park Drive, Port Washington, NY 11050-9980 (800-372-4346)

MRI (magnetic resonance imaging) machine: **$1 million**
However, some machines may cost up to $2 million. A CAT scanner costs from $350,000 to more than $1 million.

Neurological hammer (chrome): **$2**
Used by physicians to test reflexes.
Source: A&K Surgical Supplies, 135 Mamaroneck Ave., Mamaroneck, NY 10543 (800-381-1265)

18-inch surgeon's forceps: **$7.50**
Depending on their size, forceps range from $7.50 all the way down to 80 cents (for a 3 ½-inch pair). (Surgical blades are also inexpensive: sold in boxes of 100 for $15, they cost less than most razor blades.)
Source: A&K Surgical Supplies, 135 Mamaroneck Ave., Mamaroneck, NY 10543 (800-381-1265)

• • •

Malpractice insurance (annual cost) for   **$117,000**
orthopedic surgeons in Nassau and
Suffolk Counties in New York:

If the surgeon sees patients 6 hours a day, 5 days a
week, for 50 weeks a year it amounts to $78 per hour.

It Pays to Advertise

There are dozens of ways to get your message across. Whether you choose to shout it through a megaphone, emblazon it in the sky, or lay it out in an attractive display in Playboy *magazine, it pays to advertise. Of course, it costs to advertise, too.*

Mailing list of 313,000 millionaires (with phone numbers): $25,040

Specialized mailing list of over 300,000 high-income consumers. You may purchase any or all of the list (with a $200 minimum order) for 8 cents per listing. Lists are available of almost every conceivable cross section of potential consumer: urologists (9,704 names), automobile owners, by make and model of car (60 million names), jewelry designers (5,018 names), ice cream parlors (16,713), and so on. Advertising mailing lists organized by geographical region are also available. Prices for names range from 5 cents to 13 cents apiece, depending on whether you buy labels, cards, diskettes, etc.
Source: American Business Lists, P.O. Box 27347, Omaha, NE 68127

Full-page ad in *Playboy* magazine: $80,860

Exposes you to 3,402,630 avid subscribers.

• • •

Full-page ad in the *New York Times* $66,528
(Sunday edition):
Weekday rate is $55,440. Regular advertisers pay less.

Product placement in a movie: $5,000
In the early 1980s, a new and very lucrative form of advertising was born when some films began to feature brand-name products as props—for a price. Generally, companies pay $5,000 to $100,000 to get a product prominently featured in a movie. The price depends on how conspicuously the product is displayed, how "big" the movie is, and how well the film targets the audience the advertiser is trying to reach. (In 1989, Philip Morris paid a staggering $350,000 to have Timothy Dalton as James Bond smoke a single Lark cigarette in the film *Licence to Kill*.) Deals are usually negotiated by a Hollywood broker or agent who may even get the product placed for no charge, as part of a "tie-in promotion" in which the advertiser features the movie as part of a sweepstakes, coupon offer, or TV ad. Research shows that viewers are twice as likely to remember products seen in movies, as compared to ads.
Source: Baldoni Entertainment, 2811 Wilshire Blvd., Suite 510, Santa Monica, CA (310-829-2203)

An official Olympic "corporate" sponsorship: $40
For the 1996 summer games in Atlanta. **million**

Cost to produce a national TV ad (average): $196,000
Some commercials, with lavish special effects and big-name stars, may cost well over $1 million to produce.
Costs also vary according to the type of commercial it is: for example, ads for office equipment and computers average $393,000, while ads for household products average only $133,000. Some of the major cost components in a TV ad include the director's fee ($15,000), actors ($2,000 each), and a musical jingle ($22,000). Ads filmed in Los Angeles generally cost 26% more than those made in New York.
Source: American Association of Advertising Agencies, 666 Third Ave., New York, NY 10017-4056

Air time for a 30-second TV commercial on $310,000
Murphy Brown:

Air time for a 30-second commercial on the last $200,000
Tonight Show **with Johnny Carson:**
Ad rates for the May 22, 1992, show were about five
times the normal rate for a *Tonight Show* spot.

Air time for a 30-second commercial on
Channel One (classroom television): $198,000
Channel One is a daily 12-minute news program broad-
cast by satellite to over 12,000 of the nation's class-
rooms. Channel One guarantees its advertisers a
captive audience of more than 7 million young viewers.

Your ad in lights in Times Square: $1,000
$40 per minute with 25 spots per week minimum on
the famous Times Square Sony sign.
Source: Sony Video One (212-768-0301)

1,000 buttons printed with your own message: $235
For 1,000 buttons imprinted with one-color ink.
Source: Mr. Button Products, Inc., P.O. Box 68359A, In-
dianapolis, IN 46268 (800-874-7916)

Aerial banner advertising (1 hour) over Chicago: $545
Banner message can contain up to 40 characters.
Source: Ad Air Lines, 11249 S. Halsted St., Chicago, IL
60628 (312-785-3100)

Billboard on the Kennedy Expressway in Chicago $1,750
(monthly rental):
The monthly rental for a 20-foot by 60-foot billboard is
$1,750–$2,500. Approximately 150,000 cars a day (4.5
million a month) drive by the sign.
Source: Patrick Media Group Inc., 737 N. Michigan
Ave., Chicago, IL 60611 (312-573-1000)

Searchlight: $9,000

Of the type traditionally used for grand openings. These carbon-arc searchlights are World War II surplus, 6 feet in diameter, and have 800 million candlepower. New searchlights (four-beam, Xenon bulb type) cost about $31,500.

Source: Southern Outdoor Promotions, Marietta, GA (800-447-6780)

Megaphone: $79.95

Hand-held battery-powered megaphone has an 800-foot range.

Source: M-F Athletic Co., P.O. Box 8090, Cranston, RI 02920 (800-556-7464)

Last Wishes

Who'd have thought there were so many unusual—and expensive—ways to take one's final bow? It can cost as much to die well as to live well, but if there's one advantage to going out in style, it's that you don't have to see the final bill.

All the materials needed to embalm one body: **$18.66**
Includes two plastic eye caps (9 cents each), two metal mouth closure needles (8 cents each), two 16-ounce bottles of concentrated arterial fluid ($2.56 each), two 16-ounce bottles of fluid conditioners to modify strength of arterial fluid ($2.58 each), two 16-ounce bottles of cavity fluid to fill the chest and abdomen ($2.35 each), one Tro-Car button to close necessary incision between the abdominal and chest cavities (6 cents), thread for incisions (3 cents), and one 8-ounce bottle of shampoo and disinfectant to clean the body ($3.25). Does not include mortician's labor or overhead.

Makeup and hairstyling for a corpse: **$92**
The average amount charged by funeral parlors in the U.S.

Funeral home crematorium: **$35,900**
Single-body model reduces a corpse to ashes in 2 ½ hours. Installation is $5,000 to $10,000 extra. Among the accessories frequently purchased by funeral homes are a "cremains processor" (which grinds the cremated remains into uniform fragments) for $2,750, and

a "three-body refrigerator" (which stores corpses pending cremation) for $4,495.
Source: All Crematory, P.O. Box 39482, Cleveland, OH 44139 (216-248-3500)

Cadillac (or Lincoln) hearse: $60,000
A fully appointed, cheaper Buick Roadmaster station wagon hearse costs only about $35,000.
Source for Cadillac hearse: Superior/S&S Coach Co., Lima, OH (800-367-5161)
Source for Buick hearse: Images Coaches, Warsaw, IN (800-662-5342)

Mummification of a human corpse: $24,000
The body is soaked for several months in a patented preservation fluid, then wrapped in gauze, sealed in latex rubber, wrapped in layers of fiberglass, and covered with an epoxy-like resin. For another $36,000 and up, the body can be sealed in a mummiform and placed in a bronze sarcophagus (filled with inert gas to retard decomposition), with the deceased's likeness sculpted onto the lid. Mummification of pets is also available for $2,500–$7,000.
Source: Summum, 707 W. Genesee Ave., Salt Lake City, UT 84104 (801-355-0137)

Full-body cryonic suspension in liquid nitrogen: $29,500
The minimum cost. The American Cryonics Society recommends establishing an additional $20,000 trust as a fail-safe measure to ensure perpetual maintenance. Other programs cost as much as $150,000 for whole-body suspension, or $50,000 for the head only (neuro suspension).
Source: American Cryonics Society, P.O. Box 1509, Cupertino, CA 95015 (800-523-2001)

Solid mahogany pet casket: $1,000
Backyard Burials offers a wide variety of pet caskets and grave markers, plus 150 different cremation urns for animals, from $24.99 to $1,600. Grave markers

range from $14.99 for an aluminum memorial to $900 for a granite and bronze marker with vases and space for multiple name plates. A pet's photo can also be printed on a special aluminum plate that's guaranteed to last 20 years.
Source: Backyard Burials, Inc., Pittsburgh, PA (412-766-8404)

Burial plot for a large dog: $495
Prices vary depending on the size of the animal. Includes opening and closing of the grave.
Source: Mount Vernon Meadow Pet Cemetery, Whitemarsh, PA (215-828-1417)

Cremation for a cat (or a small dog): $155
$205 if the animal weighs more than 60 pounds.
Source: Alabama Pet Cemetery, Birmingham, AL (205-870-5010)

Burial plot (human) at Forest Lawn Memorial Park, Glendale, California: $1,420
For a standard burial plot in the main part of the cemetery. Secluded garden plots cost more, up to $7,800 depending on size and location.
Source: Forest Lawn Memorial Park, Glendale, CA (213-254-7251)

36-ton granite gravestone in the shape of a Mercedes-Benz limousine (life-size): $250,000
This particular tombstone was made to order for the grave of a 15-year-old boy in Linden, New Jersey.

Burial at sea: $70
The Burials at Sea Society of Pasadena, California, will conduct a small ceremony and spread cremated remains up to 3 miles out into the Pacific Ocean. They will scatter remains anywhere requested in the world, but prices vary according to location. Burial services with family and friends in attendance on the boat are

extra ($270 to $375, depending on the day of the week).
All prices include a memorial floral arrangement.
Source: Burials at Sea Society, 732 North Fair Oaks
Ave., Pasadena, CA 91103 (800-974-4244)

Set of blueprints to build your own casket: $9.95
Source: Direct Funeral Services, 2530 Santa Clara Ave.,
Alameda, CA 94501

The Animal World

Have a dog who you think might be the next Lassie? Own a cat with a bad heart? Looking to have your pet cow stylishly groomed? The number of ways you can spend money on animals is almost as varied as the animal world itself.

Acting lessons for a dog: **$4,150**

The Kamer Canine College in Los Angeles offers the 8-week course, which includes room and board. However, the dog must have first successfully completed an Advanced Obedience Course ($2,800) before starting acting lessons.
Source: Kamer Canine College, 13249 Sherman Way, North Hollywood, CA 91602 (800-252-6377)

Puppy kindergarten, 4-week course: **$1,200**

For puppies 3 ½ to 5 months old. Course includes training in basic commands, as well as consultation on behavioral problems such as chewing. "Apart from genetic influences, it is the positive experiences that the puppy has during his early months that will shape his personality, character, and lifetime temperament."
Source: Hollywood Dog Training School, 10805 Vanowen St., North Hollywood, CA 91605 (818-762-1262)

Gold dental crown for a dog: **$600**

The cost ranges from $600 to almost $900. A root canal for a cat or dog usually costs between $165 and $350.

Source: Deer Creek Animal Hospital, Denver, CO (303-973-4200)

Pacemaker for a cat or a dog: $800
More than 1,000 cats receive pacemakers annually in the U.S. The procedure sometimes costs more than $1,000. Other major surgical procedures available for cats and dogs include brain tumor surgery ($2,000), radiation therapy for cancer (12 treatments, $1,500), hip replacement surgery for dogs ($1,700–$2,000), aortic stenosis resection (fixing a heart murmur—$1,500–$2,000), the implantation of a prosthetic eye ($400–$800), and kidney transplants for cats ($2,500–$3,500). The procedures are done by some veterinary schools like Colorado State University and the University of California at Davis, as well as some specialized private clinics such as the Animal Referral Center at Fountain Valley, California.

A guide dog for the blind: $30,000
Estimated total cost for the 8- to 10-year working life of the dog, including training, student instruction, follow-up, and lifetime care of the dog. Trained guide dogs are provided at no cost to qualified blind persons through the appropriate agencies.
Source: Guide Dogs for the Blind, San Rafael, CA (415-499-4000)

A video for cats: $19.95
"*Video Catnip* is a video filled with birds, squirrels, chipmunks, and nature sounds that will have your cat running and jumping toward your TV screen." The same company, Pet Avision, is working on a video for TV-watching birds.
Source: Pet Avision, P.O. Box 102, Morgantown, WV 26507 (800-822-2988)

A bat house: $29.95
The equivalent of a birdhouse for bats. Will house 5–15 bats. A larger bat house (for 50–70 bats) is $89.95. "Made from rough-cut untreated Texas cedar . . . Bats

love them!" Touted as the natural way to eliminate mosquitos: "Bats eat up to 600 mosquitos per hour!"
Source: Vida Products, Inc., P.O. Box 549, Spring, TX 77383 (713-367-5075)

Stuffing and mounting a moose head: $600
The procedure takes about 6 months. Purchaser must supply moose head.
Source: Wild West Taxidermy, Colorado Springs, CO (719-591-0217)

Stuffed and mounted (synthetic) moose head: $80
Faux big game trophy is actually a stuffed animal made of soft, durable synthetic fur with leather accents, made to be mounted on a wall. Each one has the "look and feel of the real thing, with the pleasant knowledge that they're not." Twenty different kinds of big game trophies are available—including elephants, polar bears, and Holstein cows—priced from $45 to $90.
Source: Colorado Wool Works, Ltd., P.O. Box 4, Lyons, CO 80540 (800-424-7695)

Scorpion: $14.98
Live, poisonous scorpion. Sold only to schools (for use in science or nature classes), or to qualified businesses with a legitimate interest. Includes care instructions.
Source: Carolina Biological Supply Co., 2700 York Road, Burlington, NC 27215-3398 (800-334-5551)

10,000 honeybees: $29
3-pound packet of bees includes one young laying queen bee. Bee gloves are a handy accessory at $12.67 a pair.
Source: Wilbanks Aviary, Claxton, GA (912-739-4820)

• • •

Quart of (live) ladybugs: $25
A quart contains about 18,000 ladybugs. Ladybugs are
frequently purchased as an alternative to chemical in-
secticides, since they help control unwanted pests in
the garden.
Source: The Bug Store, 4472 Shaw Blvd., St. Louis, MO
63110 (314-773-7374)

Chimpanzee (6-week-old): $25,000
From an ad in a 1993 issue of *Animal Finders' Guide.*
Another ad offers Bengal tigers for $1,000–$1,500 and
snow leopards for $5,000–$7,000. Rare and endangered
animals are sold through classified ads and increas-
ingly popular exotic animal auctions. The laws govern-
ing the trade in endangered species (including
chimpanzees) are full of loopholes. For instance, the
federal government has no jurisdiction over intrastate
transactions, and certain hybrids such as the "liger"—
a cross between a lion and a tiger—are frequently not
covered under the law at all. As for technically non-
endangered animals (such as lions, cougars, and ze-
bras), it is perfectly legal to own them so long as there
is compliance with state and local laws (such as zoning
ordinances). Most of these animals, once purchased,
suffer troublesome fates, often at the hands of inept
and ill-equipped owners; some have been known to
wind up at private hunting "preserves" within the
U.S., where wealthy marksmen pay exorbitant funds to
"bag" a long-sought trophy.

Renting an African lion (or leopard, or tiger) $1,000
for 1 day:
An elephant rents for $2,000 per day, a rare black rhino
for $5,000. Carl Larsson of Florida's Circus Larsson
says he can furnish any kind of animal, even a cobra—
if the price is right. Generally, exotic animals are
rented for promotional purposes (such as commercials
or movies), but individuals can also rent them for
theme parties and birthday celebrations. One Palm
Beach couple spent $50,000 for an African safari-
themed birthday party for their daughter. Also avail-

able for rent are antique circus wagons and calliopes ($2,000–$3,000 a day for 2 or 3 wagons).
Source: Circus Larsson, P.O. Box 1632, N. Miami, FL 33261 (305-895-1333)

Hybrid Siberian white tiger and Bengal tiger: $45,000
This is the value placed on the animal (named "Blanca") by the U.S. government. Special permits are needed to own and transport tigers. This young female was confiscated at the Mexican border by U.S. Customs officials. She was in the backseat of an automobile. Blanca now resides at the San Diego Zoo.

Albino ball python: $35,000
For an extremely rare baby snake, which grows to 6–8 feet in length. An albino red tail boa costs $80,000 for a baby; it grows to 10–17 feet in length. Both snakes are white with an orangish tint. Several organizations are currently working to ban the trade in all rare and unusual reptiles and birds as a result of controversy over their treatment by some distributors and owners.

Frozen bull semen (1 vial): $11
The average price for a vial of Holstein bull semen, frozen in liquid nitrogen. The semen can be stored this way (in anticipation for eventual use in breeding) for years. Semen from bulls with especially desirable characteristics can sell for as much as $125 per vial.

Texas Longhorn (breeding female): $1,000
Bulls especially prized for their genetics bring anywhere from $1,000 to $30,000 or more.

Texas longhorn skull (with horns): $199
For a skull with a 5- to 6-foot span.
Source: Desert West Skulls, P.O. Box 10334, Prescott, AZ 86302 (602-772-4255)

Cow grooming (shampoo, haircut, and styling):   **$50**
The service is available at fairs and shows where the
animals are exhibited.

"Plainsman" saddle: **$1,250**
"Handcrafted on a Bullhide Tree, using the finest Hermann Oak Leather." Complete kit is $1,595 and in-
cludes saddle, old-time brow headstall, cowboy breast
collar, batwing chaps, military saddlebags, and rifle
scabbard. Items are priced for plain leather; carving is
extra.
Source: Hermann Oak Leather Co., P.O. Box 567, New
Palestine, IN 46163 (800-783-7996)

Steel horseshoes (pair):   **$1.85**
Dozens of varieties—in steel, aluminum, and rubber—
are available for $1.85 a pair and up. Shoes for draft
horses run $12–$13 per pair.
Source: Centaur Forge, Ltd., P.O. Box 340, Burlington,
WI 53105-0340 (414-763-9175)

A reindeer (male calf):   **$2,000**
A female calf costs about $800 more, and a fully
trained (halter-broken) adult costs $5,000–$6,000. Flying Deer Ranch at Old Snowmass, Colorado, has the
largest herd of reindeer in the lower 48 states. (Most
reindeer reside in Alaska, Canada, Russia, and the
Scandinavian countries.) Only about 1,000 of them ex-
ist in the continental U.S.
Source: Flying Deer Ranch, Old Snowmass, CO (303-
927-4621)

A carrier pigeon: **$100**
For a championship-quality English carrier pigeon.
Their smaller counterpart, the racing homer pigeon, is
much more popular with breeders. Like the carrier pigeon, the racing pigeon can find its way home from 1,000
miles or more, at an average speed of about 40 mph.

Zoo Doo fertilizer (manure from zoo animals),   **$4.95**
1-pound tub:
Or 15 pounds for $15.95.
Source: Zoo Doo Compost Co., 281 E. Parkway North,
Memphis, TN 38112 (901-276-1200)

Pooper scooper service for 1 dog (per month):   **$19.50**
Plus $12 for each additional dog.
Source: Pooper Scooper, 430 Blueridge Drive, Dun-
canville, TX 75137 (214-283-4514)

Big Machines

For all the grown-up kids who've ever wanted to own their own (full-size) locomotive, submarine, cement truck, or excavator, here's the scoop.

Garbage truck: $99,000

Heil brand top-of-the-line 25-cubic-yard packer/compactor mounted on a Mack 350-horsepower diesel tandem axle truck. The complete unit weighs about 30,000 pounds—empty. The packer/compactor alone costs $38,000.

Cement truck: $96,000

A Premier booster-style Rex Mixer (with a capacity of 10 ½ to 11 cubic yards of concrete) mounted on a diesel tandem axle truck chassis. Fully loaded, the truck weighs about 70,000 pounds. The mixer alone costs $35,000.

Railroad locomotive: $1.4 million

Heavy-haul 4,000- to 4,400-horsepower diesel/electric freight locomotive, weighing approximately 200 tons. The cost, in some instances, may run as high as $2 million. Passenger locomotives generally cost $2.3 million–$2.7 million. The major locomotive manufacturers are Republic Locomotives, General Motors, and General Electric. Republic is currently developing a high-speed turbine drive passenger locomotive capable of speeds up to 150 mph. The expected cost is $5 million.

There are 18,004 locomotives in service in the U.S., all of them diesel/electrics. The last year any steam locomotives were operated by a major railroad in the U.S. was 1980.

Railroad boxcar: $50,616

Average cost for a freight-carrying rail car. An average car can carry up to 89.3 tons (about four times what a semi-truck can legally haul).

80 feet of steel rail: $979

Price does not include track-laying expenses. A transcontinental, 3,000-mile set of tracks would use about $400 million worth of rail. An 80-foot section of rail weighs 3,627 pounds.

Greyhound-type commercial bus: $260,000

Diesel-powered Motor Coach Industries Model 102C3 holds 47 passengers, and is equipped with a bathroom.

School bus: $33,142

The price paid by Florida school districts for a new 65-passenger school bus. An individual who wished to buy the same bus would pay about $10,000 more. The price is also higher (about $47,000) in states with colder climates and mountainous terrain (such as Colorado or Utah) where buses are required by law to include heaters, extra insulation, and air brakes.

48-passenger submarine: $3.5 million

Complete, ready-to-go passenger submarine holds 48 passengers plus 3 crew members, is 65 feet long, and has an inside diameter of 7 feet. Electrically powered, it can operate at depths of up to 150 feet, and cruise at speeds approaching 2.5 knots. The submarine has porthole windows for passenger viewing, and is pri-

marily used for tourism in places like Hawaii, Guam, and the Caribbean.
Source: Atlantis Submarines, 55 West 8th Ave., Vancouver, B.C., Canada V5Y 1N1 (604-875-1367)

3-passenger submarine: $39,750
The Reef Ranger "wet" submarine is battery powered, has a top speed of 3.5 knots, and dives to a depth of 120 feet. However, it must be operated with diving gear and oxygen tanks, since the passenger compartment fills with water as part of its diving operation.
Source: Submersible Systems Technology, Inc., 3612 Reese Ave., Riviera Beach, FL 33404 (407-863-3446)

1 tire for a Boeing 747: $3,691.37
Goodyear's main gear tire for a Boeing 747-400 has an outside diameter of 49 inches. The plane uses 16 main and 2 nose tires. The tires have a useful life of about 560 individual takeoffs and landings.

Goodyear's biggest tire: $30,000
The tire, a 50/80-57, is used on giant Caterpillar front-end loaders. It weighs 9,328 pounds (by comparison, the average passenger car tire weighs only 22 pounds), is almost 12 feet high and more than 4 feet wide, and has a tread depth of 3.8 inches. A single tire is capable of carrying a 198,500-pound load.

John Deere excavator: $333,368
The John Deere 992D-LC diesel-powered excavator weighs almost 98,000 pounds. Its track shoes are 30 inches wide and 17 feet 11 inches long. The digging arm has a 40-foot reach and can dig to a depth of almost 27 feet. The unit can be equipped with various buckets, grapples, and magnets (for lifting metals). A 2 ¾-cubic-yard bucket costs an extra $12,775.

• • •

World's largest crane:

$12 million

Lamson's LTL-2500 is the largest capacity mobile crawler crane in the world. The self-propelled machine can lift up to 2,500 tons. It can be equipped with 460 feet of main boom, plus a 240-foot jib, for a total hook height of about 700 feet.

Double-hulled oil tanker:

$75 million

A supertanker measures the length of four football fields and weighs 400,000 tons. It can transport over 100 million gallons of crude oil. Double-hulled tankers cost about $15 million more than single-hulled tankers, but they're much less likely to spill oil. (Exxon Corp. spent $2.5 *billion* to clean up the Alaska coastline after the single-hulled *Exxon Valdez* spilled 11 million gallons of crude oil in 1989.)

Oil spill containment boom (1,000 feet):

$12,000

The 18-inch boom is made of PVC, like the material in a raincoat, but of much heavier construction. Each boom is composed of a 6-inch float and a 12-inch underwater skirt, which contains the oil. By law, facilities that unload oil from ships must have at least 1,000 feet of containment boom on hand in case of disasters. Containment booms made of fireproof materials can cost ten times as much. They're used when an oil spill is burned off.
Source: IG Environmental, Houston, TX (713-999-4422)

Mack semi-tractor/truck:

$85,000

An "18-wheeler" consists of a tractor/truck (cab and engine) and a trailer (see below). A new Mack tractor/truck with a 350- to 500-horsepower diesel engine costs from $85,000 to $105,000 without trailer. The complete rig with trailer usually weighs 30,000–40,000 pounds empty. Fully loaded, the truck and trailer can weigh up to 80,000 pounds (the legal gross weight limit on most highways).

•   •   •

3 types of semi-trailers—

—48-foot refrigerated truck van: $40,500
Great Dane's 48-foot-long (by 8 ½ feet wide) "reefer"
van with a Thermo-King refrigeration unit. The trailer
weighs 14,300 pounds. A standard box or "dry" van of
the same size runs $16,500.

—48-foot flatbed trailer: $15,000
All-steel sliding tandem trailer with toolbox and
winches. Trailer weighs 11,000 pounds. An alu-
minum/steel composite trailer weighs 1,000 pounds
less, but costs $4,000–$5,000 more (the less the truck
and trailer weigh, the more cargo it can haul without
exceeding legal load limits).

—9,500-gallon fuel tank trailer: $48,000
Onnen Tanker has 4 fuel compartments ($53,000 for a
5-compartment tanker). The trailer is 42 feet long and
weighs 9,200 pounds. The tanker loads fuel at the rate
of 650 gallons per minute. Safety features include double bulkhead, vapor recovery system, and overfill protection system.

Pierce Aerial Ladder fire truck: $400,000
Models can run as high as $500,000, depending on
how they're equipped. They're powered by a 450- to
500-horsepower engine, the ladder extends 75 to 105
feet, and they're painted bright red (unless a customer
requests a different color—lime green is also popular).
The Pierce 100-foot Platform truck with basket costs
from $500,000 to $600,000. The Pierce Responder, a
pumper truck with a 500-gallon tank capable of pump-
ing 1,000 gallons of water per minute, costs anywhere
from $100,000 to $350,000.
Source: Pierce Mfg. Co., Appleton, WI (414-832-3000)

Erector set: $179.95
Deluxe version with 540 parts contains instructions for
75 different building projects, including a chairlift, a
radar station, and a jet fighter. Smaller erector sets
start at $15.95.
Source: World of Science, 900 Jefferson Road, Bldg. 4,
Rochester, NY 14623 (716-475-0100)

Compellingly Commonplace

Remember when $3,000 would buy a nice house? Now all it will buy is a phone booth—without the phone. On the other hand, you can still get a 4-wheel moving vehicle for under $100—even if it is a grocery shopping cart.

Phone booth, glass enclosed $3,000

Booths are constructed of stainless steel and tempered glass, have a bi-fold door, and come fully assembled. The actual phone is extra. A deluxe-model phone booth—reinforced with double stainless steel, sound-proofed, and equipped with seat, lighting, ventilator, and ashtray—can cost as much as $6,000. Reproductions of quaint "Old English"-style wood and glass phone booths cost about $2,800 each.

Source: Redy-Ref Pressed & Welded, Long Island City, NY (718-784-3690)

Pay telephone (wall mounted, AT&T): $1,095

Installation costs an additional $170.

30-foot telephone (or power) pole: $115

Made from Western red cedar. A 40-foot pole costs $185.

Parking meter (mechanical): $200

Mechanical variety with knob that must be turned after coin is deposited. Pole not included.

Source: POM, Inc., Russelville, AR (501-968-2880)

Fire hydrant: $1,100

Standard, 6-foot "bury hydrant," meaning that 6 feet is buried in the ground, with 3 feet rising above ground. The aboveground portion has a "dry barrel" so that the unit does not freeze.
Source: East Jordan Iron Works, East Jordan, MI (616-536-2261)

Stop sign: $50

Standard stop sign, measuring 30 inches by 30 inches. Price does not include post.
Source: Midwest Barricade, Colorado Springs, CO (719-392-3461)

Traffic stoplight: $270

Standard traffic light with 3 light signals—red, yellow, and green. Includes lenses, lightbulbs, and housing.

Traffic signals for a 4-way intersection: $32,000

Installed price includes 8 sets of lights, 8 sets of pedestrian signal heads, 4 push buttons, span wire construction, and vehicle detection system. More elaborate systems (such as those with lights suspended from metal mast arms instead of overhead wires) cost about $80,000 installed.

Street sign (with street name on both sides): $19.50

Post not included.
Source: Midwest Barricade, Colorado Springs, CO (719-392-3461)

Men's bathroom urinal (wall mounted): $156

Made of vitreous china, this is the least expensive wall-mounted urinal made by Kohler. A flush valve assembly is about $150 more. A top-of-the-line 4-foot-high floor-mounted urinal costs $502.

• • •

Electronic gasoline pump: $11,000
Deluxe high-volume pump dispenses gasoline from 6
hoses, 3 on each side.

Manhole cover: $78.35
26-inch cover weighs 146 pounds. The frame for the
manhole cover weighs 246 pounds and costs $117.65.
Source: East Jordan Iron Works, East Jordan, MI (616-
536-2261)

Department store mannequin (female): $846
Fully equipped with glass base, rod, decorated face,
and wig. Male mannequins cost $16 less because they
have shorter hair.
Source: Decter Mannikin, Inc., Los Angeles, CA (213-
627-9842)

Barber pole: $539.50
Lighted pole is 28 inches high with a 6-inch-diameter
glass cylinder. A 2-light barber pole, 47 inches high
with an 8-inch cylinder, runs $759.50.
Source: WIlliam Marvy Company, 1540 St. Clair Ave.,
St. Paul, MN 55105 (800-874-2651)

Supermarket shopping cart: $50
Heavy-duty models can cost as much as $125.
Source: Unarco Commercial Products, Oklahoma City,
OK (405-232-2431)

Supermarket checkout scanner: $5,000
IBM system includes scanner, cash register, display,
computer, and controller. The system is usually connected to a larger, and more expensive, main store
computer.

•   •   •

Automatic teller machine (ATM): $16,000
NCR state-of-the-art lobby machine. Drive-through
systems (which require separate structures to house
them) are more expensive. Basic models like the ones
found in convenience stores start at about $9,000.

School chalkboard (4 feet by 8 feet): $133
Board is made of green slate with aluminum frame
and a chalk tray along the base.
Source: Colborn School Supply Co., Denver, CO (303-
778-1220)

12-inch-high theater marquee letters (each): $12.80
To have enough letters to spell almost any message,
you need about 98 letters—$1,254 worth. A set of 12-
inch theater rating symbols—X, G, R, PG, PG-13—
costs a total of $166.10.
Source: Gemini Inc., 103 Mensing Way, Cannon Falls,
MN 55009-0018 (800-LETTERS)

Judge's gavel (11 inches, American walnut): $10.50
This is the wholesale price; the retail price is approximately twice that. Bulk discounts are available: for example, buy 250 gavels, and the wholesale price drops
to $8.65 apiece. (The idea of buying gavels in bulk isn't
far-fetched. The Gavel Company's brochure touts the
idea of using them as giveaways: "50,000 gavels were
sent by a pharmaceutical company to doctors throughout the country asking them to *judge for themselves*
when comparing the company's products to a
generic.") The Gavel Company also sells expensive,
boxed "presentation sets," which include the gavel, a
sound block, and a jeweler's bronze engraving band.
The suggested retail price for a boxed set can run as
high as $209.
Source: The Gavel Company, 203 Northfield Road,
Northfield, IL 60093 (800-4-GAVELS)

• • •

Exit sign $22.40

There are more elaborate and expensive models, but
this is the standard lighted steel exit sign.
Source: Grainger (800-225-5994)

Objets d'Art

It is said that a thing of beauty is a joy forever. Unfortunately, in the realm of fine art, you may be paying for it forever, too.

6-foot ice sculpture of a panther: $750
Sculptures are hand-chiseled at room temperature and last about 10 hours. Renowned L.A. ice sculptor Rex Covington will also do smaller ice sculptures (4 feet high or so) for $175.
Source: Ice Sculptures by Rex Covington, Los Angeles, CA (213-937-8485)

Lalique crystal table: $35,750
"Three Lionesses" coffee table stands just over 16 inches high, with a circular glass top 48 inches in diameter. The rounded base is composed of 4 panels—carved intaglio against a satin-finished background, in the Lalique tradition—portraying lionesses drinking from a jungle stream. Another, more expensive Lalique table—the "Cactus" table—stands 30 inches high, weighs nearly 1 ton, and costs $74,500.

Robert Mapplethorpe photograph: $7,500
Prices vary from $7,500 for a silver gelatin print to about $25,000 for a platinum print. Prices also vary according to the availability and demand for certain photos. (Most of Mapplethorpe's work was printed in limited editions of 10.) Mapplethorpe's controversial

erotic photographs do not necessarily cost more than his others.

Source: Robert Miller Gallery, 41 East 57th St., New York, NY 10022 (212-980-5454)

Ansel Adams print, *Moonrise, Hernandez, New Mexico* (circa 1941): $16,000

16- by 20-inch silver gelatin print of one of Adams's most famous photographs: the moon rising over Hernandez, New Mexico. Adams's prints range in cost from $3,000 to about $20,000. Mural-size prints are also available for as much as $100,000. For more limited budgets, the Ansel Adams Gallery sells 8- by 10-inch prints of 30 images of Yosemite for $125 each. They're made from the original negatives and printed by a former assistant of Adams.

Source: The Ansel Adams Gallery, P.O. Box 455, Yosemite National Park, CA 95389 (209-372-4413)

Having your portrait done by a renowned portrait artist: $25,000

Portraits, Inc. of New York City is an agency/gallery that represents many leading portraitists: Herbert Abrams, Marshall Bouldin, William Draper, Peter Egeli, E. Raymond Kinstler, Thomas Loepp, John Howard Sanden, and Aaron Shikle, among others. The price range is $25,000 to $50,000 (but can be as high as $100,000) for a three-quarter figure (from the knees up). Head-and-shoulder portraits are somewhat less, full figures a bit higher.

Source: Portraits, Inc., 985 Park Ave., New York, NY 10028

Life-sized wax figure of yourself: $10,000

Price is for a complete life-sized wax figure, naked except for the genitals and buttocks. Clothed portions of a wax figure are made of mannequin parts while the skin is wax; therefore, the more skin that shows, the more expensive the figure. A wax figure that consisted only of the head and the hands (with the rest of the fig-

ure clothed) would cost less, from $4,000 to $7,800.
Source: Hollywood Wax Museum, 6767 Hollywood
Blvd., Los Angeles, CA 90028 (213-462-5991)

Waterford crystal chess set with mahogany case: $12,500

18th-century Crystal De Baccarat chandelier: $45,000
Chandelier is circa 1760 and is 6 feet high, 4 feet
across, and has 60 lights. Renee Talbot French Antiques of Los Angeles has a wide selection of imported
chandeliers ranging in price up to about $80,000.
Source: Renee Talbot French Antiques, 8404 Melrose,
Los Angeles, CA 90069 (213-653-7792)

3-tier chandelier: $10.99
"Turn an ordinary lightbulb into a beautiful three-tier
chandelier! Make your home a castle without putting
out a fortune." Small, plastic chandelier attaches
around base of lightbulb. Postage and handling are $3
extra.
Source: Sterling/Macfadden, Dept. CHAN MWG, 35
Wilbur St., Lynbrook, NY 11563.

Norman Rockwell *Saturday Evening Post* cover, $99,000
original oil painting:
The painting of a hat-check girl—which appeared on
the cover of the 3 May 1941 *Post*—sold at auction in
1993 for $99,000. A 24 May 1948 cover painting, *Happy
Skiers on a Train,* sold for $132,000 in 1993. $240,000 is
the record auction price for one of the 322 covers Rockwell painted. An original Rockwell sketch can be
bought for as little as $1,000, and a limited-edition
signed reproduction of one of his paintings for
$2,500–$9,000. The Norman Rockwell Museum in
Stockbridge, Massachusetts, exhibits over 100 Rockwell paintings and sketches (including his first *Post*
cover, *Boy with Baby Carriage,* from 1916). Price of admission is $8.
Source: Norman Rockwell Museum, Stockbridge, MA
(413-298-4100)

A Michelangelo drawing: **$6.32 million**

The drawing *The Holy Family on the Flight into Egypt* was purchased at a Christie's auction in 1993 by the J. Paul Getty Museum in Malibu, California. The sale broke the previous record price for an Old Master drawing, which had been previously held by Leonardo da Vinci's *Drapery Studies*, sold in 1989 for $5.8 million.

A Picasso drawing: **$36,300**

"*The Death*," a 1903 drawing of a murderess staring down at her victim, sold at Sotheby's in 1993.

A Jackson Pollock oil painting: **$827,500**

Sold at a Christie's auction in 1993 and titled *Number 26, 1951*, the painting was described by the *Wall Street Journal* as "a big, black, powerful amoeba of paint." That same year, an earlier Pollock—titled *Number 19, 1948*—sold for $2.4 million.

Van Gogh *Sunflowers* oil painting: **$39.9 million**

The 1889 painting, one of a handful of sunflower paintings done by Van Gogh, was sold in 1987 at Christie's in London. The price set a record for a painting at auction. The current record price of $82.5 million was set by another Van Gogh masterpiece, *Portrait of Dr. Gachet*, in 1990.

A Monet "water lilies" oil painting: **$12.1 million**

Monet's *Waterlily Basin* was auctioned at Christie's in New York City in 1992 for $12.1 million.

Painting by Ruby the elephant: **$1,000**

Ruby, an Asian elephant, resides at the Phoenix Zoo, where she has become famous for the colorful and unusual pictures she paints holding a brush with her trunk. $1,000 is the minimum price for one of Ruby's 16-inch by 20-inch acrylics (up from $250 just 4 years ago). The Phoenix Zoo sells at least a dozen of her paintings every year, and there is currently a 3-year waiting list

for one of her pictures. Dick George, who has written Ruby's biography, says the paintings are abstract—"to *us* they certainly are, but who knows to an elephant." Ruby selects her own colors from a palette held by a zoo employee, and her paintings have been known to mirror various objects (a certain color car, a certain color coat) within view while she's working.
Source: Phoenix Zoo, Phoenix, AZ (602-273-1341)

Audubon print *Carolina Turtledove* (1833):   **$9,350**
Print measures 25 ⅞ inches by 20 ⅝ inches.

A Little Learning

You, too, can join the ranks of thousands who have exciting and high-paying careers in brain surgery, bartending, and household management. A mind is a terrible thing to waste.

Bartending school, 40-hour course: $450

The Seattle School of Mixology offers 40 hours of training in how to become a bartender, including classes in proper drink preparation, interpersonal communications skills, and how to handle the "overserved" customer.
Source: Seattle School of Mixology, 166 Denny Way, Seattle, WA 98109 (206-441-3838)

High school diploma (by mail): $399

Home study course covers grades 9–12, and takes 9 months to 2 years to complete; 4 to 5 hours of study per week is suggested. Exams are open book.
Source: ICS Newport/Pacific High School, 925 Oak St., Scranton, PA 18515 (800-992-8765)

A 10-page pre-written term paper: $75.00

Research Assistance has papers on over 19,000 topics, from "U.S.-Greece Relations after WWII" (17 pages) to "Fellini: Childhood and Films" (10 pages) to "Dioxin Contamination of Seveso, Italy, in 1976" (8 pages). The company advises that "all reports sold to students are

for research purposes only." Term papers cost $7.50 per page up to a maximum of $127.50 for any one report. Research Assistance promises to mail your order within 4 hours after you call them, and will even ship papers overnight for an extra fee.
Source: Research Assistance, 11322 Idaho Ave., Suite 206, Los Angeles, CA 90025 (800-351-0222)

The 20-volume unabridged *Oxford*   **$2,750**
English Dictionary:

The Art and Science of Dumpster Diving (book):   **$16.95**
Written by John Hoffman, this 152-page book "will show you how to get just about *anything* you want or need—food, clothing, furniture, building supplies, entertainment, luxury goods, tools, toys—AB-SOLUTELY FREE!" All from Dumpsters.
Source: Loompanics Unlimited, P.O. Box 1197, Port Townsend, WA 98368

Encyclopaedia Britannica, 32-volume 1992 edition: **$1,199**
Standard edition. The exclusive Edinburgh Edition (limited to 100 subscribers) comes bound in the finest blue leather with gold trim, and costs $10,000. Outdated *Britannica*s tend to lose their value rather dramatically: a 1964 edition can be bought at used bookstores for about $40.

The New York Times on microfilm   **$190,975**
(1851 to the present):
The price for 1994 alone is $1,840.

SAT (Scholastic Assessment Test) prep course: **$495**
The Kaplan Educational Centers claims that students who take their full course increase their SAT scores by an average of 115 points.
Source: Kaplan Educational Centers (800-KAP-TEST)

1 year of medical school (tuition and fees): $29,440

Price is for 1 year of tuition and fees at George Washington University Medical School, the most expensive in the U.S. Tuition and fees for all private medical schools average about $20,000 per year. Tuition has increased at several times the rate of inflation over the past several years; as a result, there have been calls to freeze or even reduce tuition rates. One school, the University of Pennsylvania, has even announced plans for zero tuition—sometime in the next century. The most expensive state-supported medical school is the University of Michigan, where 1-year tuition is $14,435, for in-state residents.

1 year's tuition, room, board, and supplies—

—at Harvard College: $26,230

—at Montana State University (in-state residents): $7,913

Berlitz "total immersion" language course in Russian: $5,600

The course runs 7 ½ hours a day, 6 days a week, for 2 weeks, and is designed to give the student basic conversational fluency. Three to four instructors are assigned to each student each day (sometimes two at a time), even during the lunch break. Berlitz offers the same "total immersion" course (at the same cost) in numerous other languages: Swahili, French, Spanish, Norwegian, Thai, and dozens more. Less expensive language courses are available: for example, group programs (with 6 to 8 students per group) cost $299 for thirty 45-minute lessons.

Source: Berlitz International, 293 Wall St., Princeton, NJ 08540 (609-497-9940)

Language course on audiocassette: $20

For do-it-yourselfers, the Living Language Basic Course (for Japanese, Italian, German, Spanish, Russian, French, or Continental or Brazilian Portuguese) is available, 30 lessons on cassette ($20) or CD ($30).

Source: Living Language Basic Course (800-733-3000)

Eight 1-hour belly dancing lessons: **$48**
Four 1-hour classes can be had for only $28.
Source: Marliza's Belly Dance School, Las Vegas, NV
(702-870-5508)

8-week course in household management: **$4,450**
The concentrated 8-week training program—offered
by Starkey International Institute for Household Management in Denver—prepares people for professional
careers in virtually all aspects of home management.
Subjects include "Household Maintenance," "Enter-
taining," "Preparing for Fine Dining," and "Valet Re-
sponsibilities."
Source: The Starkey International Institute for Household Management, Inc., 1410 High St., Denver, CO
80218 (303-394-4904)

Private detective home study program: **$199**
The 25-lesson course includes study on such subjects
as "Interviewing and Interrogation," "Auto Reposses-
sion and Lockpicking," and "Juveniles, Sex, and Drugs
(a highly profitable specialty)." Students receive their
own wallet badge, with the words "Private International Investigator" engraved on it.
Source: Global School of Investigation, P.O. Box 336,
Stoneham, MA 02180

Get Even: The Complete Book of Dirty Tricks: **$19.95**
Guide teaches basics of creative revenge: *"Get Even* is
crammed with eye-opening anecdotes of sweet revenge on roving lovers, tyrannical bosses, noisy dogs,
merciless landlords, crooked businessmen, deadbeats,
bigots, snobs, bullies, and just about any situation that
calls for getting even!"
Source: Eden Press, P.O. Box 8410, Fountain Valley, CA
92728 (800-338-8484)

Celebrity Collectibles

Who can explain the mystique of owning Madonna's negligee, Abraham Lincoln's autograph, or Mr. Spock's ears? They're more than mere investments. Even if you never make money on them, to have them in your home is to own a piece of history, and to touch them is to experience vicariously some of the glory and glamour that they reflect.

Madonna's negligee: **$24,000**
Sold in London in 1993.

Marilyn Monroe's negligee: **$7,700**
Black silk negligee, adorned with an appliqued pink rose at the bodice, worn by Monroe in the 1952 movie *Niagara*.

Papal carpet (one swatch):   **$1**
1 square inch of carpet that Pope John Paul II walked on during the 1993 papal Mass in Denver: "This carpet has not been cleaned—being fresh from the Mass itself."
Source: Bylina, P.O. Box 9211, Albuquerque, NM 87119 (505-265-2551)

Abraham Lincoln's autograph   **$2,000**
For a plain signature—the least valuable type of autograph. Autographs of any historical figure or celebrity are progressively more valuable if they appear on a photo, a typed letter or document, or a handwritten

manuscript or letter. "Content in autographs is equivalent to location in real estate," adds Bob Erickson, president of the Universal Autograph Collectors Club. The way an autograph is "packaged," and who sells it, also makes a difference. Autographs that come beautifully framed or marketed at a flashy store sell for considerably more than does an unframed item purchased from a simple dealer. Likewise, an autograph that's in excellent condition will often fetch a premium. A top-notch Lincoln signature could bring as much as $6,000. Other historical autographs and their minimum prices: Howard Hughes ($1,000), Albert Einstein ($800), Charles Dickens ($600), and John Hancock ($1,500).
Source: Richard Kohl, 1840 North Federal Highway, Boynton, FL 33435 (800-344-9103)

Tom Cruise's autograph   **$150**
Other celebrity autographs and their prices: Frank Sinatra ($600), Marilyn Monroe ($1,000), Brooke Shields ($175), Jimmy Durante ($100), *Lost in Space*'s June Lockhardt ($50), and *Batman*'s Adam West ($40).
Source: Kronakos, 9201 Washington St., Denver, CO 80229 (303-457-2612)

The Colt Cobra .38 revolver used to kill   **$220,000**
Lee Harvey Oswald:
The gun was sold at auction in 1991. The man who bought it is now trying to recoup his investment by shooting bullets through it (into a barrel of water to prevent disfiguration) and selling the bullets for $1,495 apiece. Each bullet comes framed with a certificate of authenticity.

Toe tag from the corpse of Lee Harvey Oswald: **$8,000**
Sold at a recent auction.

Alex Haley's Pulitzer Prize: **$50,000**
Awarded to Haley in 1977 for *Roots: The Saga of an American Family*. The prize was sold at auction in 1992,

to satisfy the late author's debts. It was the first Pulitzer Prize ever to be auctioned off.

"Dan Quayle for U.S. Senate" button (1980): **$15**

Richard Nixon "I am not a crook" wristwatch: **$195**

Vivien Leigh's Best Actress Oscar for **$563,500**
Gone with the Wind:
The Oscar brought more than twice the expected price when sold at auction in December 1993. Denouncing the resale of Academy Awards as "a vulgar business," the Academy of Motion Picture Arts and Sciences has required winners in recent years to sign an agreement stipulating that if they ever decide to dispose of their Oscar, the Academy has the first right to purchase it for $10. However, this provision has been largely ignored or circumvented, and Oscars usually bring a hefty price when they come on the market. The Academy will not disclose their actual cost for an Oscar, but $300 is the replacement (and insurance) value assigned in instances where an Oscar is lost by fire, flood, or other natural disaster. Each award stands 13 ½ inches high, weighs 7 pounds, and is composed of pewter with gold electroplate.
Source: Collectors Bookstore, Hollywood, CA

Marlon Brando's Best Actor Oscar for **$13,500**
On the Waterfront:
Brando received his Oscar for *On the Waterfront* in 1954. He reportedly used it as a doorstop before giving it to a friend. The price of $13,500 was considered a bargain at the time the Award was sold in 1988.

Orson Welles's script (first draft) for *Citizen Kane:* **$50,000**
Sold at auction in 1993.

•   •   •

Signed group photo from *The Andy Griffith Show:*   **$500**
Photo depicts and is signed by Andy Griffith, Don
Knotts, Jim Nabors, and Ron Howard.
Source: Kronakos, 9201 Washington St., Denver, CO
80229 (303-457-2612)

Transcript of the first murder trials of Lyle and   **$13,093.50**
Erik Menendez:
The 26,187-page transcript—of the 1993 murder trials
of Lyle and Erik Menendez (which ended in hung ju-
ries)—costs 50 cents per page. It's available to anyone
wishing to purchase it from the court reporter at Van
Nuys, California.
Source: Court Reporter, Superior Court of the State of
California, City of Los Angeles, Van Nuys Branch (818-
374-3189)

Mao Tse-tung gold pocket watch: **$19,388**
Available in Beijing in limited quantities (only 99 were
made), the watch displays the image of Mao in platinum, and is adorned with 36 diamonds, a ruby, and 4
sapphires. The watches range from $17,888 to $19,388.
(Ones with "lucky" serial numbers are the most expensive.) For about $10, the budget-minded can buy a
basic Mao wristwatch (with Tiananmen Square visible
in the background).

Mickey Mouse wristwatch (diamond encrusted):   **$6,900**
Available on Main Street U.S.A. at Disneyland.

Joan Rivers's shoes: **$1,000**
Her size 7 Manolo Blahnik's were sold at an AIDS ben-
efit auction held at Barney's, the upscale New York
clothing store.

Red slippers worn by Judy Garland in   **$165,000**
The Wizard of OZ:
Sold at auction in 1988, the slippers brought a record
price for a pair of shoes.

Munchkin costume from *The Wizard of Oz*: **$660**
Gold felt and cotton vest with covered buttons from
the 1939 classic.

Pair of Mr. Spock's ears: **$1,100**
The ears were worn by Leonard Nimoy in the 1984
movie *Star Trek III: The Search for Spock,* and come with
a note of authenticity from Nimoy as well as an autographed photo.

Baseball autographed by Babe Ruth: **$2,750**

Baseball bat autographed by Mickey Mantle: **$8,250**

Basketball autographed by Magic Johnson: **$399**

Michael Jordan's jersey: **$20,900**
The jersey worn by Jordan at the University of North
Carolina in 1982 was sold at auction in 1993.

Hockey stick autographed by Wayne Gretzky: **$195**

Captain Kangaroo lunch box, vinyl (1964–66): **$325**
A complete Captain Kangaroo lunch box, containing
the original Thermos, is one of the more expensive col-
lectible lunch boxes. A vinyl Barbie lunch box (from
between 1962 and 1964) usually sells for $45–$85.

Roman gold coin depicting Julius Caesar: **$20,000**
Coins depicting Brutus (Caesar's assassin) can fetch
over $160,000. Gold coins of the Caesars usually sell
for $2,500 to $25,000, depending on condition and
which emperor is depicted.

Roman coin of Antony and Cleopatra: $6,000
From the 32–1 B.C. period, the coin depicts Cleopatra
on the obverse side and Marc Antony on the reverse.
Source: Tom Cederlind, P.O. Box 1963, University Station, Portland, OR 97207 (503-228-2746)

And the Penalty Is . . .

Indeed, almost everything does have a price. This applies even to trouble, which can be bought with all too much ease. However, the price of an illegal activity is set not by the law of supply and demand, but by the law of the land. You may pay as little as $2 for the "privilege" of jaywalking in downtown Manhattan, or as much as a cool million for polluting the (already significantly polluted) Hudson River.

Maximum fine for parking illegally overnight in Tokyo: **$1,400**

Parking ticket in New York City (maximum fine):   **$55**

The maximum fine is for especially serious offenses, such as parking in front of a fire hydrant or at a bus stop. If the offender's car is towed, there's an additional $150 towing charge, plus storage costs. Parking fines are slightly higher south of 96th Street in Manhattan than elsewhere in the city. The minimum parking fine in New York City is $25.

Fine for jaywalking in New York City: **$2**

The law is not generally enforced, however.

A false alarm in Denver: **$50**

The first two false alarms of your home burglar alarm system are free, but after that the police charge $50 each time they have to respond to the alarm.

Maximum fine for auto theft in Massachusetts: **$15,000**
Plus up to 15 years in state prison. The thief (or the receiver of the stolen vehicle) must also pay restitution of
damage or financial loss.

Fine for driving while intoxicated (DWI) in   **$3,500**
South Carolina (third offense):
South Carolina is the state with the highest mandatory
minimum fine for a drunk driving conviction on the
third offense. However, Iowa and New York have the
highest fine for a first offense—$500.

IRS penalty for failure to put your social security   **$50**
number on your income tax return:

Maximum fine for dumping hazardous wastes   **$1**
Plus prison term of up to 15 years for violation of the   **million**
Resource Conservation and Recovery Act (RCRA).

Maximum fine for violations of the   **$70,000**
Occupational Safety and Health Act (OSHA):
Per violation.

Maximum fine under U.S. law for—

—Wearing a uniform of the U.S. armed forces,   **$250**
without authority:
Plus 6 months' imprisonment, or both.

—False weather report: **$500**
If the false report is represented as coming from the
U.S. Weather Bureau. Plus 90 days in jail, or both.

—Intimidation of voters: **$1,000**
Plus 1 year in prison, or both.

—Stowing away on a ship or plane: **$1,000**
Plus 1 year in prison, or both.

—Impersonating a foreign diplomat: **$5,000**
Plus 10 years in prison, or both.

—Selling a person into slavery: **$5,000**
Plus 5 years in prison, or both.

**Average fine (and restitution) imposed by
U.S. courts for—**

—Murder: **$5,640**

—Kidnapping, hostage taking: **$80,461**

—Money laundering: **$182,564**

Maximum fine in Alabama for possession   **$2,000**
or use of drug paraphernalia:
For first offense—a Class A misdemeanor, carrying a
maximum fine of $2,000 and maximum jail term of 1
year.

Maximum fine for performing an animal   **$1,000**
sacrifice in Los Angeles:

Fine for appearing bare-chested or in a   **$24**
swimsuit on the streets of Venice, Italy:

Law and Order

Keeping criminals at bay (and defending yourself if you're accused of being one) can be a costly proposition. Just ask the FBI, or the Menendez brothers.

"Police line do not cross" barrier tape   **$14.95**
(1,000-foot roll):
Made of heavy-duty yellow vinyl, 3-inch width.
Source: Quartermaster, 750 Long Beach Blvd., Long
Beach, CA 90813 (800-444-8643)

Police radar gun: **$850**
Hand-held stationary unit. More sophisticated models
that operate while the police cruiser is in motion cost
about $1,150.
Source: Central Equipment Co., Millis, MA (508-376-
2951)

Wooden billy club: **$11.50**
Collapsible batons are about $55.
Source: Central Equipment Co., Millis, MA (508-376-
2951)

Trained police dog: **$3,000**
Includes the cost of training. However, the price does
not include the cost of training the police officer to
handle the dog.

Source: Central Equipment Co., Millis, MA (508-376-2951)

New York City police officer's uniform: $500

Head-to-toe, a complete street uniform costs $500 to $700, including leathers. A complete dress uniform runs about $1,500.
Source: Frielich Police Equipment Inc., 211 East 21st St., New York, NY 10010 (212-254-3045)

Light bar for police cruiser: $400
Price does not include installation.
Source: Central Equipment Co., Millis, MA (508-376-2951)

Automobile boot (immobilizer): $335
Wheel immobilizers for automobiles range from $335 to $495. A motorcycle "immobilizer" costs about $265, and for semi-trucks a "boot" costs $855.
Source: Miti Manufacturing Co., 3183 Hall Ave., Grand Junction, CO 81504 (303-434-9100)

Alcotest breath test kit: $950
Hand-held battery-powered device used by police departments measures Breath Alcohol Concentrations after a subject blows into a tube connected to the unit. A portable printer that prints up the test results costs an additional $950.
Source: National Draeger, Inc., P.O. Box 120, Pittsburgh, PA 15230-0120 (412-787-8383)

Armored car: $55,000
Brinks and Wells Fargo types of armored cars are custom-made to the specifications of the buyer, and they usually cost from $55,000 to $60,000.
Source: Pro-Tech Armored Products, Pittsfield, MA (800-234-3104)

• • •

Hand-held metal detector: **$229.95**
Source: Central Equipment Co., Millis, MA (508-376-2951)

Walk-through metal detector: **$3,995**
The kind used in airports.
Source: Central Equipment Co., Millis, MA (508-376-2951)

X-ray baggage and parcel examination unit: **$28,000**
As used in airports. The basic unit produces black-and-white images. A color image unit is about $20,000 higher. A unit capable of specifically detecting a wide variety of explosives costs around $125,000.
Source: Control Screening, Greensburg, PA (800-343-9727)

"Bionic ear" (listening device):   **$109.50**
Pole-type, "magnifying" microphone. "Hear conversations and animal noises up to 100 yards away." With a parabolic booster kit (a small, satellite-type dish that attaches to the microphone)—$129.45.
Source: Quartermaster, 750 Long Beach Blvd., Long Beach, CA 90813 (800-444-8643)

Body wire and receiver set: **$299**
Of the type used to "wire" informants. As advertised in *Soldier of Fortune* magazine.

Body wire detector: **$695**
Detects whether or not a person is "bugged." To detect bugs transmitted at very low frequency over power lines requires other sophisticated—and expensive—equipment. A phone "tap nullifier," costing about $695, jams telephone taps. This body wire detector and the body wire (above) are much less expensive than similar professional models.
Source: Executive Protection Products, Inc., 1325 Imola Ave. W. #5045, Napa, CA 94559 (707-253-7142)

Night vision goggles: $5,850

Some less sophisticated night vision equipment can cost as little as a few hundred dollars.

Source: Excalibur Enterprises, P.O. Box 400, Fogelsville, PA 18051-0400 (215-391-9106)

Your FBI and CIA records: $35

Infomedia of Washington, D.C., can obtain your FBI, CIA, NSA, DoD, state records, and more.

Source: Infomedia, Suite 376, 2020 Pennsylvania Ave., N.W., Washington, DC, 20006

Paper shredder: $2,595

High-quality office shredders capable of handling 15 to 55 sheets at a time start at $2,595 and run up to $3,795. They'll even shred staples, paper clips, and Acco fasteners along with the paper. High-volume conveyer-fed shredders, with capacities of 750 pounds to 3 ½ tons per hour, cost from $8,495 to $32,995.

Source: Allegheny Paper Shredders Corporation, P.O. Box 1897, Fairfield, IA 52556 (800-345-8585)

$100,000 bail bond (in Detroit): $10,000

Fees are generally regulated by each state. In Michigan, prices are fixed at 10% of the amount of the bond. The bonds are good for up to 1 year, after which the bonding company charges an extra premium. The bonding company may or may not require collateral, depending on how creditworthy the applicant is.

Source: A-1 Bail Bonds, Detroit, MI (800-475-1450)

Hourly fee for a lawyer at a top New York law firm: $500

The big-name firms generally won't discuss it for publication, but fees of $500 to $600 per hour are not uncommon.

An "expert" witness for a lawsuit (per day): $400

The classified-ads section of the *ABA Journal* and other lawyer magazines are filled with ads for specialists in "bad faith," "accident reconstruction," "seatbelt claims," "toxic exposure," and "warning labels," among others. These specialists tout their experience, "presentation skills," and credentials ("on prestigious university faculty")—all of which will affect their credibility in front of a jury. A Colorado consultant on wood products charges $50 per hour for investigative forensics work; for depositions and court testimony—$800 a day. A document examiner from Chicago charges $150 per hour. A neurologist from Boston gets $250 per hour. Expenses, such as travel, are always extra. The best experts are those who are experienced, but not "shopworn"—meaning they haven't testified in so many trials as to appear to be a professional "hired gun" who's willing to say anything for a price.

A voice I.D.: $1,525

An audio expert compares two voices to determine if they are the voice of the same person. An authenticity determination (audio or visual) to check whether a tape has been edited or tampered with costs $2,525. Tape enhancement (to improve clarity) runs $200 per hour.
Source: Owl Investigations, Inc. (800-OWL-AUDIO)

Filing fee for U.S. Supreme Court appeal: $300

The Court can waive this fee in cases of financial hardship.

An appeal to the U.S. Supreme Court (legal fees): $100,000

If the Supreme Court agrees to hear a case (most appeals are rejected), the legal tab usually runs $100,000–$140,000, according to Farr, Smith & Taranto, a Washington, D.C., law firm that specializes in Supreme Court appeals. However, the firm sometimes takes cases on a contingency fee basis or, in special cases, works *pro bono.*
Source: Farr, Smith & Taranto, 2445 M St. N.W., Washington, DC, 20037 (202-775-0184)

• • •

Becoming a "card-carrying" member of the ACLU: $20
A joint membership costs $30, a limited-income membership $5.
Source: American Civil Liberties Union, 132 West 43rd St., New York, NY 10036

An Ounce of Prevention

Hindsight is almost always clearer than foresight, but it is also a lot more expensive. A root canal can cost hundreds; a roll of dental floss is less than $2. A smoke detector will set you back only about $10; a catastrophic fire can drive you into bankruptcy.

50 yards of dental floss: **$1.49**
Johnson & Johnson dental floss, waxed, mint flavored.

1 condom: **67 cents**
Trojan brand latex, lubricated with nonoxynol-9. Box of 12 for $7.99.

A smoke detector: **$9.99**
First Alert smoke detector, 9-volt battery included.

Deadbolt lock: **$13.99**
Single cylinder, for doors without windows.

Insect repellant, 6-ounce can: **$4.99**
Cutter brand aerosol insect repellant.

1 birth control pill—Ortho Novum: **78 cents**
Prescription calls for 1 tablet per day. The generic equivalent, Norethin, costs 43 cents per pill.

Bullet-proof vest: $275
Capable of stopping bullets of up to .38 caliber. Vests
for higher "threat levels" can cost up to $1,000.
Source: Central Equipment Co., Millis, MA (508-376-
2951)

How to Legally Hide Your Money in $10
Switzerland **(booklet):**
Source: Eden Press, P.O. Box 8410, Fountain Valley, CA
92728 (800-338-8484)

10-minute call to La Toya Jackson's Psychic $39.90
Network:
"Our world-famous psychics are available 24 hours a
day."
Source: La Toya Jackson's Psychic Network (900-420-
1227), $3.99/minute.

Having a chimney cleaned (in Stowe, Vermont): $40
Add $10 to clean the fireplace or stove as well.
Source: Chimney Care, Stowe, VT (802-244-6166)

Hard hat: $5.01
Basic model. More protective and durable hard hats
are available for more money.
Source: W. W. Grainger, Inc. (800-225-5994)

Fire insurance in Malibu, California, for $3,400
$1 million home (average annual premium):
All-risk homeowner's policy (earthquakes and floods
excluded), with a $500 deductible. Includes $750,000
coverage for contents.

Earthquake insurance for a $500,000
home (average annual premium)—

—in Los Angeles: $1,135

—in Pueblo, Colorado: **$175**

The rate in L.A. is $2.27 per $1,000 of coverage, with a 10% deductible. In Pueblo (where the last significant earthquake was over 150 years ago), the premium is 35 cents per $1,000, with a 5% deductible.

Home Sweet Home

Whether it's a home in Bel Air or a simple tipi, your home is your castle—all for a fee.

10-story elevator (installed): $120,000

State-of-the-art traction elevator. An old-style hydraulic elevator in a 5- to 10-story building would cost about $42,000. In either case, the price listed assumes that certain things are already in place: a hoist way (elevator shaft), a machine room, and the right kind of power. Elevators for buildings with 30 or more floors require more sophisticated equipment. As a rule of thumb, elevator installation runs about 10% of the total construction cost of a new high-rise building.

Washing all the windows in the Empire State Building (cost of labor): $26,622

Until the Empire State Building recently replaced its 6,500 windows with swing-in type windows (which can be cleaned from the inside), it took 3 men 2 months to wash the outside of all the windows (after which they started all over again). At about $17 per hour wage, plus $8.50 per hour for workman's insurance and fringe benefits, the labor cost was more than $25,000.

Escalator: $80,000

For an escalator with a 20-foot rise, the installed cost is $80,000 to $100,000. At top speed, the maximum capacity is 9,000 people per hour, assuming 2 people per step. Since most people in the U.S. don't like to be that close together, 3,600 per hour may be a more realistic capacity estimate. Washington, D.C., is perhaps the most escalator-intensive city in the U.S.—the subway system alone has more than 500.

Moving walk (airport style): $125,000
The installed cost for a moving walk, 100 to 150 feet in length. Some moving walks are significantly longer, such as the 430-foot moving walk at the Pittsburgh airport. Most moving walks travel at about 150 feet per minute (less than 2 miles an hour).

Office space in the World Trade Center $42,000
(1,000 square feet for 1 year):
Rent on larger offices may be negotiable. No space is available above the 77th floor.

A mansion in Bel Air: **$19 million**
On 1.6 acres. Features 18th-century paneled rooms and almost a dozen imported fireplace mantels. Inspired by a chateau of Louis XIV just outside Paris. A mansion, unlike a mere house, should have a name. This one's is "La Lanterne."
Source: *Immobilier International,* the magazine for properties of international interest

A plantation in Tennessee: **$15 million**
1,550-acre working farm, with an imposing 16,000-square-foot residence at its heart. House facade features 10 Corinthian columns. The home also comes furnished with a wealth of antiques from the period 1845–65.
Source: *Immobilier International,* the magazine for properties of international interest

• • •

A vineyard in Sonoma, California: **$6.5 million**

A 5,000-square-foot home on 140 acres. The $200,000 vineyard income won't quite make the house payment.
Source: *Immobilier International,* the magazine for properties of international interest

A ski chalet in Aspen: **$6.5 million**

12,000-square-foot mountaintop estate, with a panoramic view of the ski slopes and downtown Aspen. The average home in Aspen costs $1.2 million. Prices are so high that the community has instituted a "deed restricted" affordable housing program for local residents, such as doctors, who can't afford million-dollar homes. Because of this, some apartments and houses are available in Aspen in the $40,000–$185,000 range.
Source: *Aspen Magazine* [holiday issue, 1993–4]

A hacienda in Santa Fe: **$4.2 million**

2-acre compound located in the historic Old Town section of Santa Fe features a 7,000-square-foot adobe main residence, 2 guesthouses, a lavish swimming pool, and a tennis court.
Source: *Immobilier International,* the magazine for properties of international interest

A thoroughbred horse farm in Kentucky: **$3.95 million**

Besides the 5,500-square-foot main residence, the 342-acre property is fully equipped to breed and train thoroughbred horses. (The horses are not included.)
Source: *Immobilier International,* the magazine for properties of international interest

A showplace in Las Vegas: **$3.9 million**

Las Vegas mansion has 16,000 square feet; 7 bedroom suites (the master suite alone has 2,268 square feet), fireplaces, Jacuzzi, chandeliers, marble throughout. Right next to a golf course.
Source: *Immobilier International,* the magazine for properties of international interest

A castle in France: **$2.95 million**
Historic castle sits on 125 acres of rolling French countryside. The exterior is adorned with turrets, spires, and handcrafted sculptures; the interior has been modernized, and comes fully furnished.
Source: *Immobilier International,* the magazine for properties of international interest

A penthouse atop Manhattan: **$1.75 million**
3-bedroom penthouse has 3,200 square feet of living space, a 1,500-square-foot roof garden, and some of the best views in the city.
Source: *Immobilier International,* the magazine for properties of international interest

A colonial farmhouse in New Jersey: **$675,000**
Built in 1780, and enlarged in 1840, this completely updated farmhouse sits on 5.7 beautifully landscaped acres.
Source: *Immobilier International,* the magazine for properties of international interest

A villa in Spain: **$380,000**
Located on Ibiza Island, and overlooking two bays, this Moorish villa has 1,600 square feet of living space.
Source: *Immobilier International,* the magazine for properties of international interest

House in Honolulu: **$361,747**
Median price for a single-family home. Honolulu has the highest median price for resale of single-family homes of any city in the U.S. New homes average $430,749.

1,800-square-foot home in Pueblo, Colorado: **$80,225**
The lowest average price for homes out of 306 urban areas surveyed by the ACCRA.

A tipi: $275
Panther Primitives has tipis from $275 for a 12-foot model up to $1,198 for the 24-footer with flame retardancy. The book *Painted Tipis* ($10) contains excellent ideas for decorating the plain canvas.
Source: Panther Primitives, P.O. Box 32, Normantown, WV 25267 (800-487-2684)

80-foot by 80-foot pole tent: $64,000
Clear-span pole tent with aluminum frame and PVC vinyl-coated materials. As a rule of thumb, the cost for larger tents is $10 per square foot (with sides included). A much smaller tent—800 square feet, polyester, star-shaped, center-pole canopy style—runs $3,650.
Source: Hawker (813-482-8004) and KD Kanopy (800-432-4435)

Parking attendant's booth: $5,200
Plus about $1,000 for installation. The 4-foot by 6-foot booth (half steel, half glass) has heating and air-conditioning.
Source: Par-Kut International, Harrison, MI (800-394-6599)

Highway tollbooth: $41,000
Constructed with stainless steel and tempered safety glass, the 6-foot by 12-foot booth is the type found on the Pennsylvania Turnpike. Installation and equipment (such as automatic toll collectors) will increase the price to about $100,000.
Source: Par-Kut International, Harrison, MI (800-394-6599)

Wrecker's demolition ball (16,000 pounds): $19,414.60
The 48 ½-inch-diameter ball is the largest made by Frederick Foundry & Machine. For smaller jobs, their 15-inch wrecking ball (weighing 470 pounds) costs $755.04.
Source: Frederick Foundry & Machine, Frederick, MD (301-663-1020)

Demolition of an 8-story, 80,000-square-foot   **$640,000**
apartment building in New York City:
Assumes building is brick and steel construction, not
reinforced concrete. Removal of any asbestos or PCBs
is extra.
Source: Invirex Demolition, Inc., Huntington Station,
NY (516-673-0007)

After a Fashion

Decisions, decisions. Granny boots or combat boots with that snappy little Halston original? A tuxedo or black leather overalls to the Oscars? Dressing up or dressing down—if you're truly fashionable, money should be no object.

Santa Claus suit: $400
Custom-made velvet suit includes coat, hat, belt, pants, and boot covers. However, white wig and beard cost $60 extra. The whole costume can usually be rented for about $55 a day.
Source: Costume Country, Englewood, CO (303-761-8281)

Clown costume (rental for 3 days): $90
Authentic clown costume in blue and red, with gold lamé. Wig and makeup are included.
Source: Adele's of Hollywood, 5034 Hollywood Blvd., Los Angeles, CA 90027 (213-663-2231)

"Hillary wig," with detachable hairband: $175
Source: Jacquelyn Wigs, 15 West 37th St., New York, NY 10018 (212-302-2266)

Elevator shoes for men: $69.95
A hidden inner mold adds about 2 inches to the wearer's stature (up to 3 inches on some pairs of boots).

Offered in a wide variety of styles. Prices range from $69.95 to $145.
Source: Richlee Shoe Company, Frederick, MD (800-343-3810)

Lighted bedroom slippers: $34.95

Both slippers have small "headlights" (which project light up to 12 feet ahead) built into the front tips of the soles. Lights run on AA batteries, which are included.
Source: Hammacher Schlemmer, Operations Center, 9180 Le Saint Drive, Fairfield, OH 45014-5475 (800-543-3366)

Granny boots: $550

Lace-up revivals of turn-of-the-century footwear are offered in suede or velvet, and are available at better department stores. "Boots are the answer to everything," says designer Donna Karan.

Bronzed baby shoes: $19.99

You supply your baby's first shoes and they will be bronzed forever in solid metal. Mounting costs extra and engraving is 35 cents per letter.
Source: American Bronzing Co., P.O. Box 6504, Columbus, OH 43272-8568

Tuxedo from Bernini in Beverly Hills: $1,500

$1,500–$1,600 for their best tuxedo.
Source: Bernini (800-BERNINI)

Black leather overalls: $349.95

"Farmer-style. Fun to wear." A leather bandanna ($19.95) completes "the rustic look."
Source: The Pleasure Chest, 7733 Santa Monica Blvd., West Hollywood, CA 90046

• • •

Harley-Davidson suspenders: **$9.99**
2-inch-wide black suspenders have orange "Harley-
Davidson" lettering.
Source: The Sportsman's Guide, 411 Farwell Ave.,
South St. Paul, MN 55070-0239 (800-888-3006)

Complete set of 50 state trooper patches: **$210**
Or single patch for $4.95. Also available are police de-
partment patches for 50 cities from Juneau to Tallahas-
see—single patch ($4.95) or set of 50 ($210).
Source: Quartermaster, 750 Long Beach Blvd., Long
Beach, CA 90813 (800-444-8643)

Union officer's uniform from the Civil War: **$9,500**
Original "K.I.A. 69th Penna. Uniform" includes coat,
trousers, and cap—all in near perfect condition. An authentic officer's sword to go with it costs $1,850 extra;
an 1863 Enfield rifle/musket costs $1,950.
Source: David W. Taylor, P.O. Box 87, Sylvania, OH 43560

Stetson "100X El Presidente" hat: **$1,100**
By comparison, Stetson's least expensive hat, a 4X
model, costs a little over $100. Prices vary from dealer
to dealer. The "X" designates the amount of beaver fur
used in the hat: the higher the number, the better the
quality. Stetson has been outfitting America's best-
dressed cowboys since 1865.

Men's felt Amish hat: **$49.98**
Black Dynafelt, 3-inch brim, sizes 6 7/8 through 7 1/2.
An authentic Amish bonnet for women costs $39.98.
Source: Kidron Town & Country Store, 4959 Kidron
Road, Kidron, OH 44636

Authentic Soviet Army winter hat: **$25**
"Warm up now that the cold war is over."
Source: Baltic Rim Trading Co., Santa Monica, CA (310-
399-0734)

Regulation Special Forces beret: $14.95
Available in several colors including Special Forces
green and dark navy blue.
Source: Quartermaster, 750 Long Beach Blvd., Long
Beach, CA 90813 (800-444-8643)

U.S. Army combat boots: $89.95
There are army boots for almost every situation: jungle
boots ($59.95), parade boots ($105), paratrooper boots
($89.50), and Special Forces waterproof boots ($114.50).
Source: Quartermaster, 750 Long Beach Blvd., Long
Beach, CA 90813 (800-444-8643)

Soul Searching

The road to heaven and the path to nirvana are lined with tollbooths. Please have your quarters ready.

Confessional booth: $400

3-foot by 3-foot portable confessional booth stands 7 feet high, and is made of solid wood. Prices range from $400 to $600.
Source: Patrick's of Bayside, 203-18 35th Ave., Bayside, NY 11361 (718-428-6727)

Church pulpit: $1,200

Solid oak pulpit, Gothic style, 3 feet wide by 1 ½ feet deep by 45 inches high.
Source: J. P. Redington & Co., P.O. Box 954, Scranton, PA 18501 (800-233-4281)

Church pew (15 feet): $625

Solid oak with built-in cushion. Since a 15-foot pew holds 10 people, a church that seats 300 would need 30 of them, or $18,750 worth. Installation is included.
Source: J. P. Redington & Co., P.O. Box 954, Scranton, PA 18501 (800-233-4281)

Solid gold rosary beads: $1,500

Beads, wire, and centerpiece are all made of solid 14K gold. Lead crystal rosary beads (from Swarovski of the Czech Republic) cost $600 to $700. The cheapest plas-

tic rosary beads can be bought for as little as 40 cents.
Source: Patrick's of Bayside, 203-18 35th Ave., Bayside,
NY 11361 (718-428-6727)

Going to church (average donation per $12.23
worshipper, per service, in the U.S.):
The National Council of Churches tracks churchgoers'
donations for 36 denominations. The average annual
donation is $425.78 per year. The True Old Calendar
Orthodox Church of Greece has the lowest per capita
annual giving by members ($35.56), and the Evangeli-
cal Mennonite Church has the highest ($1,522.18).

Jesus doll: $29.95
Doll is almost 2 feet tall, has brilliant blue eyes, and is
machine washable. "One of the big things," says Pulte
Rickard, the doll's creator, "is it makes it hard for people to deny His presence. They look across a room and
go, 'Oh, there's Jesus.' "
Source: First Fruits-Biblical Dolls (800-227-8702)

3-foot wood crucifix (with wood corpus): $500
Source: Patrick's of Bayside, 203-18 35th Ave., Bayside,
NY 11361 (718-428-6727)

A sliver of Christ's cross: $9,000
Two tiny slivers of wood reputed to be pieces of the
cross on which Christ was crucified were sold in 1993 at
a charity auction in Paris for $18,000. They had earlier
been authenticated as "relics" by the Vatican, which,
nonetheless, condemned the sale as a possible sin.

Pope scope: $8.50
As a result of Pope John Paul II's visit to Denver in
1993, legions of entrepreneurs developed and hawked
more than 300 pope-related souvenirs for the faithful.
While a few of these products were antagonistic ("Say
Nope to the Pope" bumper stickers), most were rever-
ential, such as the pope coffee mug or the commemo-

rative pope plate. One of the most popular items was the Pope Scope, a long periscope that allowed viewers to see over the heads of other people in order to get a better view of His Eminence.

Yarmulke: $1.50
Velvet yarmulkes cost $18.00 per dozen, satin yarmulkes $12.50. Source: E. Weisberg Hebrew Religious Articles, New York, NY (212-674-1770)

1-hour therapy session with Sigmund Freud $8.10
(circa 1920):

1-hour therapy session for a pet with animal $150
behaviorist Bashkim Dibra:
Dibra, who wrote *Teach Your Dog to Behave,* has many celebrity clients, including Mia Farrow, who paid to have him see her Bichon Frise, Maggie. Dibra, who lives in New York City, also conducts workshops for would-be animal actors.
Source: Bashkim Dibra, New York, NY (718-796-4341)

A battery of psychological tests: $1,000
Cambridge Counseling Associates of Cambridge, Massachusetts, will administer a package of psychological tests that form the basis for a standard personality assessment, such as a court might order a defendant to undergo. The tests are conducted over 2 or 3 sessions, and include a psychodiagnostic interview, the Thematic Apperception Test (TAT), the Rorschach inkblot test, the Bender-Gestalt, the Minnesota Multi-Phasic Personality Inventory (MMPI), the House-Tree-Person Test (interpretation of drawings), and an IQ test.
Source: Cambridge Counseling Associates, Cambridge, MA (617-868-6557)

·   ·   ·

Handwriting analysis—a personality profile: **$45**
Hugh Bickford, a Certified Master Graphoanalyst, offers a range of handwriting evaluations, from the basic personality profile (submit a 1-page sample of handwriting) to a comprehensive compatibility profile for two people for $400 (each person should submit 3 to 5 pages of handwriting).
Source: Positive Life Choices, 24552 Hawks Circle, Evergreen, CO 80439.

Tea Leaf Reading (book):   **$8.95**
Written in the early 20th century by a "Highland Seer," and published by Harney & Sons, the book teaches the basics of reading tea leaves. "Those who have the good fortune to buy it will find this book a complete guide to consulting the 'tea leaf oracle.' " Harney & Sons also distributes an excellent selection of teas by mail order.
Source: Harney & Sons, P.O. Box 638, Salisbury, CT 06068 (800-TEA-TIME)

Tour of Tibet and the Himalayas: **$9,595**
35-day trip begins in Hong Kong and travels through China to Tibet and Nepal. Among the highlights are a visit to the Temple of the Great Buddha at Leshan, a visit to Mount Emei (the highest of the four sacred mountains of Buddhism), visits to the temples and monasteries of Tibet, a tour of the Dalai Lama's Summer Palace, and visits to numerous ancient shrines and temples of Hinduism. Price includes all meals, comprehensive sightseeing, lectures, gratuities, and accommodations at luxury hotels. It does not include airfare to Hong Kong or return airfare to the U.S.
Source: Travcoa, P.O. Box 2630, Newport Beach, CA 92658-2630 (714-476-2800)

LSD (per "hit"):   **$5**
As reported in _High Times_ magazine [1994].

Everything Elvis

If he were really alive, wouldn't he come forward to claim the royalties?

Admission to Graceland: $8

Includes a tour of Elvis's 15,000-square-foot Memphis mansion, as well as an opportunity to visit his grave. The "Sincerely Elvis" museum across the street has a separate $2.75 admission.

Source: Graceland, 3764 Elvis Presley Blvd., Memphis, TN 38116 (901-332-3322)

Subscription to the *Elvis International Forum*: $14.95

4 quarterly issues, with such features as "Elvis: Our Love for Him Is True," "Elvis: Recording Rumors and Realities," and "Elvis Movies of the 50s," plus poems commemorating Elvis, and international fan club reports. Illustrated with dozens of black-and-white and color photographs, including a full-color, pullout centerfold of Elvis.

Source: *Elvis International Forum*, P.O. Box 3373, Thousand Oaks, CA 91359.

***Are You Hungry Tonight? Elvis' Favorite Recipes* (cookbook):** $12.95

Plus $2 postage and handling. "Includes his mama's recipe for mashed potatoes . . ."

Source: Lorne E. Allgood Enterprises, P.O. Box 156, Suwanee, GA 30174

The Two Kings by A. J. Jacobs: $8.95
From Bantam Books, a compendium of the amazing
but true "similarities" between Elvis, the King of Rock
& Roll, and Jesus Christ, the King of Kings. For example: "Jesus lived in a near Eastern land in a state of
grace; Elvis lived in Graceland in a nearly eastern
state." Or, "Jesus walked on water; Elvis surfed."

Elvis Presley trading cards (set of 12): $1.49

The "King Suite" at the Wilson World Hotel $52.95
(across from Graceland Mansion):
Per night for 2 people, tax not included; 2-room suite (a
living room and a bedroom) comes with refrigerator,
microwave, color TV, and king-size bed. Their motto:
"This is about as close as you can get to the King!"
Source: Wilson World Hotel, Memphis, TN (800-
WILSONS)

Hiring an Elvis impersonator: $500
Charles King of Denver, winner of the Americana International Elvis Competition, bills himself as "The
Shadow of Elvis." King charges $500 for a small gath-
ering, $1,000 for a large convention. Expenses not in-
cluded.
Source: Charles King, 1401 East Girard Ave., Englewood, CO 80110 (303-761-0976)

Elvis oven mitt: $4.99
Elvis postage stamp artwork is printed on the oven
mitt in a repeating pattern. The Elvis potholder, also
imprinted with the Elvis stamp, is $3.99.
Source: Graceland Gifts, 3734 Elvis Presley Blvd.,
Memphis, TN 38116 (800-238-2000)

Elvis Presley's American Express card: $96,000
Sold at auction in 1994.

One of Elvis's guitars: $153,000
Christie's sold the guitar in 1993.

Elvis wristwatch: $29.95
Plus $4.95 postage and handling. "Bears the same like-
ness the U.S. Postal Service recently immortalized as a
historic stamp."
Source: CT 2 Marketing, 1701 N. Heidelbach Ave.,
Evansville, IN 47711 (800-CT2-MKTG)

Elvis Christmas ornament: $6.99
"Replica of Elvis stamp is vividly reproduced on lus-
trous Glass Ball." A reproduction of Elvis's signature
appears on the other side of the 3 ½-inch ornament.
Source: Graceland Gifts, 3734 Elvis Presley Blvd.,
Memphis, TN 38116 (800-238-2000)

Original 1957 *Elvis Christmas Album:* $1,500
For one of the original RCA/Victor LPs in mint condition. Albums in less pristine condition can bring as
low as $500.

Elvis boxer shorts: $24.95
These colorful shorts are emblazoned with dozens of
Elvis images.
Source: Idols West, P.O. Box 951048, Mission Hills, CA
91395 (818-830-2787)

The Universal
Language

Did you know that a Stradivarius violin is worth the equivalent of 5,000 years of Muzak piped into your home or office? Or that $4.4 million will buy you either an original manuscript by Mozart or 1,450 accordions?

Conductor's baton: **$4.95**
The least expensive instrument in a symphony is the one that coordinates all the others. Most conductor's batons cost from $4.95 to $25, but a deluxe graphite baton can cost as much as $100.

Stradivarius violin (mint condition):   **$3 million**
Prices start at about $800,000 for a Stradivarius that has flaws.
Source: Jacques Francais Rare Violins, Inc., 250 West 54th St., New York, NY 10019 (212-586-2607)

Renting Carnegie Hall for an evening: **$11,800**
The price for renting the famed 2,804-seat concert hall includes the use of backstage personnel and a staff of ushers. However, other services—such as stage labor and lighting—are extra, and are priced according to the requirements of the performance.
Source: Carnegie Hall Corp., New York, NY (212-903-9600)

Steinway Model D, concert grand piano (walnut):   **$72,900**
Steinway's top-of-the-line piano. The same model in
ebony is $66,100. Prices for Steinway's grand pianos
start at about $25,000.
Source: Steinway & Sons, Steinway Place, Long Island
City, NY 11105 (800-STEINWAY)

Digital disk player piano (upright):   **$6,900**
Player piano uses 3 ½-inch floppy disk instead of paper rolls like the old-style player pianos. Each disk
contains 20 to 30 pieces of music, and there are 15,000
disks to choose from (including performances by
Gershwin, Rachmaninoff, etc.). A feature that allows
you to record and play back your own performances
costs an additional $1,000. A basic player grand piano
costs about $12,400, with the record and playback fea-
ture. Since a digital disk player can be installed in almost any piano, costs can vary according to the price
of the piano.

A piano concert by the winner of the Van Cliburn   **$5,000**
competition:
For a single performance by the current gold medalist.
Price includes performer's travel expenses. Silver
medalist costs $3,500, and bronze medalist $3,000.
Concerts are booked through the Van Cliburn Founda-
tion. Van Cliburn himself is also available for perfor-
mances, but will not publish his rates.
Source: Van Cliburn Foundation, 2525 Ridgmar Blvd.,
Suite 307, Ft. Worth, TX 76116-4599 (817-738-6536)

Bagpipes: **$3,000**
Top-quality Scottish bagpipes—made from ebony, and
hand-engraved and jointed with silver—consisting of
10 pieces, 2 tenors, a drone, a chanter, and a blowpipe.
Bagpipes start at about $550 for inexpensive Indone-
sian imports. However, as one might expect, the best
instruments come from Scotland.

• • •

Harp: $21,000

For Venus Harps' best concert-quality harp, the carved and gilded Centurion, constructed of maple with a spruce soundboard. The Centurion stands more than 6 feet high, has 47 strings, and weighs 77 pounds. The less expensive Cherub model weighs 68 pounds, measures 69 inches by 17 inches, and costs $7,050.
Source: Hidden Valley Harps, 1444 Calle Place, Escondido, CA 92027 (619-743-0747)

Saxophone: $3,500

For a top-of-the-line professional alto sax. A tenor sax of the same quality runs $3,800–$4,000. A baritone sax costs about $6,500.

Accordion: $3,000

Professional-quality accordions generally cost between $3,000 and $4,000, but they can be as expensive as $25,000 for a custom-made model with gold plating, mother-of-pearl keys, and an extended keyboard with 45 keys (compared to 41 on a standard full-size accordion). Very inexpensive (and much less durable) accordions can start as low as $150.
Source: Accordion-o-rama, New York, NY (212-675-9089)

Muzak in your home or office (lowest monthly rate): $50

The price of having Muzak piped into your home or office can range from $50 to $500 per month, depending on the size of your facility and the number of channels you choose. Along with the standard background music for which Muzak has become renowned, there are 11 other channels, including country & western and jazz.

***Il Duce—Mussolini's Greatest Hits* (audiocassette):** $11

40-minute cassette contains "original songs and marches of Italian Fascism, from 1922–1943."
Source: W.U.N. Enterprises (W), P.O. Box 642, New Monmouth, NJ 07748

Having 1,000 copies of your own CD manufactured: $1,750
Price does not include studio time to record your production and to make a digital audiotape master used to produce the CDs. (Recording studios in Los Angeles charge anywhere from $100 to $500 per hour.) However, it does include packaging costs, except for printing the insert and the label. Cassette tapes are even less expensive to produce: about 80 cents apiece in quantities of 1,000.
Source: Virco Recording Co., Los Angeles, CA (213-283-1888)

Musical manuscript of Mozart (in his own hand): $4.4 million
Sold at Sotheby's in 1987. The manuscript was a bound volume of 9 complete symphonies in Mozart's handwriting.

Signed portrait of Luciano Pavarotti or Placido Domingo: $350
Each in a limited edition of 100.
Source: Metropolitan Opera Guild, 70 Lincoln Center Plaza, New York, NY 10023-6593 (800-892-2525)

13-day European opera tour: $6,265
Includes round-trip airfare between New York and Milan, meals, and deluxe hotel accommodations. Includes visits to Munich, Salzburg, and Budapest. Itinerary includes at least 6 opera performances or concerts.
Source: Opera Europe, P.O. Box 1427, Pomona, CA 91769-1427

Disco mirror ball (48-inch diameter): $1,425
Not included in the price is a 22-pound rotater ($130) needed to turn the ball, and at least 4 pin-spot lights ($20 each) used to illuminate it. Small mirror balls (6–8 inches in diameter) cost only $20 or $30.
Source: Farralane Lighting & Audio Inc., 300 Farmingdale Road, Route 109, Farmingdale, NY 11735

Fog machine: $295

Fog machine creates the right ambience for a disco, magic show, or seance. The machine uses a special fluid that costs $26 per gallon (enough for about a hundred 70-second blasts of fog).

Source: Farralane Lighting & Audio Inc., 300 Farmingdale Road, Route 109, Farmingdale, NY 11735

See the World

Around the world in 80 ways. A slow boat to China, a supersonic jet, a 2-wheel bike, and a 4-wheel carriage. All major credit cards accepted. Gratuities (usually) not included.

Admission to the Louvre: **$6.61**
35 francs for adults, 20 francs for 18- to 25-year-olds and those over 60. Children under 18 are admitted free.

Admission to the museum that houses   **$3.50**
Jayne Mansfield's death car:
Officially known as "The Tragedy in U.S. History Museum," and located in St. Augustine, Florida, it displays not only the car in which sex symbol Jayne Mansfield was decapitated, but also various Kennedy assassination memorabilia (including Lee Harvey Oswald's bedroom furniture), as well as a 16th-century Spanish prison cell (complete with a human skeleton). The local chamber of commerce reportedly denies its very existence.
Source: The Tragedy in U.S. History Museum, 7 Williams St., St. Augustine, FL 32084

U.S. passport fee: **$55**
$30 for applicants 18 years of age and under. A $10 processing fee is added to all applications. Passports are valid for 10 years.

First-class passage on the Concorde from New York to Paris: $2,916

One-way fare on Air France. Round-trip costs $5,320.

17-day vacation to Antarctica: $5,595

Mini-expedition on a 38-passenger polar research vessel to Antarctica. Various landings are made via inflatable landing craft. Price does not include round-trip airfare between U.S. and Ushuaia, on the southern tip of Argentina, where the ship is boarded.
Source: Mountain Travel-Sobek, 6420 Fairmount Ave., El Cerrito, CA 94530 (800-227-2384)

18-day voyage to the North Pole: $16,900

The Russian nuclear-powered icebreaker *Yamal* takes passengers all the way to the North Pole, cutting through the Arctic ice pack (up to 16 feet thick in places) along the way. Helicopter sightseeing flights are also part of the package. However, round-trip airfare to Murmansk, Russia (where the icebreaker is boarded), is not included.
Source: Mountain Travel-Sobek, 6420 Fairmount Ave., El Cerrito, CA 94530 (800-227-2384)

First-class passage on the *Queen Elizabeth 2* from New York to Southampton: $17,520

For the most deluxe accommodations available. Per person, one-way, based on double occupancy. Price includes return airfare on the Concorde.
Source: Cunard Line, 555 Fifth Ave., New York, NY 10017-2453 (212-880-7500)

Tour of Windsor Castle: $12

Tours of Windsor Castle were previously free. However, due to political pressure, Queen Elizabeth began charging a fee for the tour to help recover restoration costs after the castle was devastated by fire in 1993.

•   •   •

Ticket on the Orient Express from London to Venice (one-way with a cabin): $1,525

"A Grand Hotel on wheels . . . There is no more romantic and luxurious way to travel to or from the world's great cities than on the Venice Simplon–Orient Express." Price includes cabin accommodations, all *table d'hote* meals (including breakfast served in your cabin), all hotel-station transfers, taxes, and gratuities. Formal attire is suggested.
Source: Abercrombie & Kent, 1520 Kensington Road, Oak Brook, IL 60521

11-day tour of China: $1,399

Departing from San Francisco. Offered by Intertour of America and advertised as "America's lowest priced tours to China," the package includes round-trip airfare, hotels, meals, and sightseeing.
Source: Intertour of America, Inc. (800-628-0110)

Amazon River expedition: $2,095

10-day excursion includes round-trip airfare from Atlanta to Iquitos, Peru. Three-deck riverboat travels about 650 miles on the Amazon. Peruvian guides, as well as a trained biologist, accompany the group.
Source: International Journeys, Inc., 11595 Kelly Road, Suite 115, Fort Myer, FL 33908 (800-622-6525)

Chartering a sailing yacht for 1 week in the Caribbean: $1,895

Weeklong charters from St. Thomas start at $1,895 (off season) for the 36-foot Sabre yacht, and range up to $4,865 (in season) for the 51-foot CYC Frers yacht. Deluxe provisions (packages containing breakfast, lunch, and dinner) are extra—$18.95 per person per day.
Source: Caribbean Yacht Charters, Inc., P.O. Box 583, Marblehead, MA 01945 (800-225-2520)

6-day bicycle tour of Nova Scotia: $1,199

Plus $109 for bicycle rental. The Nova Scotia tour is only one of dozens of itineraries offered by Vermont

Bicycle Touring. Tours are rated according to degree of difficulty. The Nova Scotia tour is "easy" to "moderate," involving 25–45 miles of pedaling per day. Packages include all necessities (accommodations, food, even a fully equipped support van).
Source: Vermont Bicycle Touring, P.O. Box 711, Bristol, VT 05443 (802-453-4811)

Passage on a cargo freighter around the world (from San Francisco):   **$7,265**

Trip takes approximately 92 days. A typical itinerary includes Japan, Korea, Taiwan, Mauritius, South Africa, Argentina, Uruguay, Brazil, Venezuela, and a passage through the Panama Canal. The maximum age limit is 79. Freighter travel is cheaper than cruise lines, and certainly more intimate: most freighters have 12 or fewer passengers (by law, vessels with 13 or more passengers are required to have a physician on board). Shorter freighter trips, to almost any destination in the world, are available; however, most freighter trips still last at least a month, even when they aren't circumnavigating the globe.
Source: Van Dyck Cruises & Tours, 1301 66th St. North, St. Petersburg, FL 33710 (800-282-5151)

Central Park carriage ride for 4 (1 hour):   **$52**

The horse-drawn carriage will take you all the way around Central Park. For those in a rush, a half-hour ride can be had for $34.
Source: Central Park Carriages, New York, NY (212-736-0680)

Fare on the New York subway: **$1.25**

Parking in Manhattan (average hourly cost):   **$10**

In the most desirable locations, the price can run as high as $14.50 an hour. Monthly rates can range from $145 (plus a $3 exit fee for storage) to $475 for space on the Upper East Side. Spots in the priciest Fifth Avenue co-ops are even higher. All parking fees are subject to an additional 18 ¼% city parking tax.

Taxi fare from Philadelphia to New York City: **$331**
If 4 passengers split the bill for the 101-mile trip, the
fare works out to $82.75 per person (tip not included).

Flying a cat from Los Angeles to New York: **$78**
One-way fare for a cat in a small kennel in the baggage
compartment. A medium-size kennel will cost $158.

Flying a human body from Los Angeles to New York: **$425**
Body must be in a coffin. Rate applies for "cargo" up
to 500 pounds. (Most corpses and coffins have a com-
bined weight of approximately 350 pounds.)

Hotel room in El Paso, Texas   **$36**
The lowest average rate of any city in the U.S.

Hotel room in Naples, Florida   **$148**
The highest average rate of any city in the U.S.

Christmastime stay in a suite at Aspen's   **$1.04**
Hotel Jerome (per minute):
During Christmas week, a deluxe suite runs about
$1,500 per day. Plain rooms are $439–$499 a day. A
continental breakfast served in your room costs $9.50
per person. Back in the 1970s, before the historic hotel
was refurbished, the room rate was about $30 per day.
In 1945, it ran 50 cents a day.
Source: Hotel Jerome, 330 E. Main, Aspen, CO 81611
(303-920-1000)

Surrey with the fringe on top: **$4,775**
2-seat horse-drawn carriage. Body is 28 inches by 70
inches, made of high-grade poplar. Pony model is
slightly smaller, and a little less expensive, at $4,650.
Cumberland General Store offers a wide selection of
buggies, including a 3-seater, a buckboard, and a
"Town & Country Delivery Wagon."

Source: Cumberland General Store, Rt. 3, Box 81, Crossville, TN 38555 (800-334-4640)

1994 Cadillac Fleetwood stretch limousine: $57,000

The Cadillac Fleetwood costs about $37,000. For about $20,000 more, the car is stretched up to 5 feet, and the interior is made over with leather seats, a television, a bar, and other amenities.
Source: Potamkin Cadillac, 798 11th Ave., New York, NY 10019 (212-399-4400)

1994 Blue Bird Wanderlodge 40-foot motor home: $471,915

Powered by a 500-horsepower Detroit Turbo Diesel, and equipped with a 300-gallon fuel tank, the elegant Wanderlodge is designed to make travelers feel at home no matter where they are. A full-size galley, bathroom, and master suite are standard.

Mercedes-Benz hood ornament: $35

An oft-stolen automobile accessory, Mercedes-Benz hood ornaments cost $35 to $45 to replace, depending on the model.

Neon lights for the underside of your car: $99

Some kits can cost as much as $400.

Miniature battery-operated XJ-S Jaguar: $14,000

Miniature drive-around model for children will hold a driver and one passenger. Jaguar made only 11 of them, including one for Princess Diana's children.

Perilous Adventure

The willingness to put one's well-being at risk for the sake of a few moments of excitement is a sign of courage. Or is it just self-indulgence? No matter, there's great fun and always a measure of risk in scaling a treacherous mountain, free-falling through space, or negotiating whitewater rapids in a tiny kayak. Thrills are made and marketed for every taste and temperament.

Hang glider: $2,490
Single-surface hang glider constructed of aircraft-quality aluminum with a 145-square-foot Dacron sail. A similar hang glider with a 205-square-foot sail costs about $300 more. And a high-performance glider with a double surface (it climbs faster and higher, but is harder to land) costs $4,200. Prices do not include a harness ($350–$650) or a parachute ($350). Hang-gliding lessons cost about $75 per session.
Source: Airsports Unlimited, 1021 Bay Blvd., Ste. S, Chula Vista, CA 91911 (619-427-3375)

Whitewater kayak: $700
$700–$800 for a plastic model, $1,500 and up for a sleek racing model made of fiberglass. Touring kayaks, used in lakes and oceans, cost about the same as their whitewater counterparts. Portable, inflatable kayaks are also available for $750–$1,100.

Source: Colorado Kayak Supply, Buena Vista, CO (800-535-3565)

Parachute: $4,500

Complete top-of-the-line system constructed to military specifications comes with tandem parachute pack and main and reserve canopies.
Source: Guardian Parachute, 3412 S. Susan St., Santa Ana, CA 92704 (714-557-8032)

Private raft trip through the Grand Canyon: $20,735

8-day, 225-mile motorized river expedition. Raft holds up to 13 fellow passengers of your choice. Trip includes all provisions, even wine with dinner. The same package for a non-private trip costs $1,595 per person.
Source: Grand Canyon Expeditions Company, P.O. Box 0, Kanab, UT 84741 (800-544-2691)

Wagon-train trip (overnight): $140

Trip covers about 6 miles of open Kansas prairie. (The original wagon trains covered approximately 20 miles a day, but the wagon master at Flinthills Overland Wagon Train says his passengers don't get up as early as the old-timers.) Meals are cooked over a campfire, and coffee is brewed in a sock. Each wagon holds up to 10 people. Passengers spend the night under the stars, but must bring their own tents. Discounts are available for children.
Source: Flinthills Overland Wagon Train, P.O. Box 1976, El Dorado, KS 67042 (316-321-6300)

Joining the U.S. Cavalry (for 3 days): $525

Participants wear the uniform of an 1870s cavalry soldier, shoot a 45-70 Springfield military carbine, ride the trails that Custer rode, and camp out on the plains of eastern Montana. Weeklong excursions are available for $1,000.
Source: Davis Creek Camp, Sarpy Route Box 940, Hysham, MT 59038 (406-665-3538)

• • •

"Branding and Weaning Weekend" on a   **$275**
cattle ranch (for women only):
"The 6,000-acre Homestead Ranch, owned and operated by a woman, with women working as cowhands,
provides an excellent setting for learning new skills,
appreciating a rural way of life. . . ." Participants help
out with feeding, checking cows for pregnancy, mend-
ing fences, and more. The ranch has several programs
available, ranging in cost from $225 to $475.
Source: Prairie Women Adventures and Retreat, P.O.
Box 2, Matfield Green, KS 66862 (316-753-3465)

Outward Bound "Dog Sledding and   **$395**
Winter Camping" wilderness course (4 days):
Outward Bound offers dozens of courses (in rock
climbing, whitewater canoeing, sea kayaking, and
more) through its 5 U.S.-based centers. "The mission
of Outward Bound is to conduct safe adventure-based
programs structured to inspire self-esteem, self-
reliance, concern for others, and care for the environ-
ment." The "Dog Sledding and Winter Camping"
course is conducted in Minnesota. Most courses are
longer and more expensive. Scholarships are offered.
Source: Outward Bound, Route 9d, RR2 Box 280, Gar-
rison, NY 10524-9901 (800-243-8520)

Tuition to U.S. Space Camp: **$500**
The nonprofit camp, run in cooperation with NASA,
has campuses in Alabama and Florida. Tuition—including room, board, and educational materials—costs
$250 to $750 for 3- to 8- day programs. Designed to be
both fun and educational, Space Camp gives participants hands-on training in astronautics without actually leaving the ground. There are separate programs
for all age groups, from grade 4 through adult, with
special programs for hearing and visually impaired
persons. "Whatever you dream, you can achieve.
SPACE CAMP is a place to give your dream wings,"
says Nichelle Nichols, "Lieutenant Uhura" of *Star Trek*.
Source: U.S. Space Camp, P.O. Box 070015, Huntsville,
AL 35807-7015

Manning a fighter plane (and engaging in a dogfight):

$599

Per person. There's a 10% discount for 2 people. No prior experience is necessary. Sky Fighters of Denver offers a 1 ½-hour orientation before participants don a military helmet, flight suit, and gloves, and jump into the front seat of a fighter plane (a *real* pilot accompanies flyers in the rear seat). The real pilot handles the takeoff and landing, but participants do most of the flying and all of the shooting. Once in the air, a dogfight begins with another plane. The entire adventure lasts about 4 hours.

Source: Sky Fighters, 7395 South Peoria, Box C11, Englewood, CO 80112 (303-790-7375)

Grand Prix racing school:

$395

5-hour program affords would-be race car drivers the opportunity to drive an open-wheeled Scandia Formula 2000 race car around a real racing track. More extensive training is available. A "Five Day Grand Prix Racing Week" costs $3,100.
Source: Bertil Roos Grand Prix Racing School, P.O. Box 221, Blakeslee, PA 18610 (800-RACE-NOW)

Climbing Mt. Kilimanjaro:

$3,570

Participants fly to Nairobi, Kenya (air transportation not included), before beginning a 16-day trek that culminates in 1 week of strenuous hiking to the 19,340-foot summit of Africa's highest mountain. Other climbing excursions (to Kathmandu, Mt. McKinley, and Mont Blanc in the Alps) are also available.

Source: Mountain Travel-Sobek, 6420 Fairmount Ave., El Cerrito, CA 94530 (800-227-2384)

Greyhound bus ticket from Seattle, Washington, to Key West, Florida:

$199

The trip takes 4 days and covers 3,900 miles.

Up in the Air

Whether it's a 747 jetliner or a hot air balloon, there are any number of contraptions and conveyances to get you off the ground. The prices are guaranteed to bring you back to earth.

Beechjet 400A, 9-passenger private jet:
$5.8 million

The Beechjet 400A has a top speed of 538 mph, a maximum cruising altitude of 45,000 feet, and can travel 2,100 miles without refueling. The cost of the fuel for a one-way flight from Los Angeles to New York would be about $1,300.
Source: Beechcraft, P.O. Box 2973, Wichita, KS 67201-2973

Boeing 747-400 jetliner:
$143 million

Boeing's largest commercial aircraft (with a wingspan of over 210 feet) seats 420 passengers, has a range of 8,290 miles, and costs from $143 million to $170 million, depending on engine selection, interior layout, and other options. By comparison, a Boeing 737-300 costs only $34 million–$40 million.
Source: Boeing Commercial Airplane Group, P.O. Box 3707, Seattle, WA 98124-2207

Sikorsky 12-passenger jet helicopter:
$6 million

The twin-turbine S-76 helicopter carries up to 12 passengers and 2 pilots, and carries a maximum gross weight of 11,700 pounds. Depending on what options a buyer selects, it can cost up to $7.5 million. The S-76

can be configured for corporate use, offshore oil use, search and rescue, or emergency medical service applications.
Source: Sikorsky Aircraft, Stratford, CT (203-386-4000)

Renting the space shuttle for a mission: **$150 million**

The Japanese Space Agency rented part of the shuttle in 1992, and paid $91 million. The Germans rented most of an entire shuttle mission in 1993, and paid $150 million.

Renting a full-size blimp (per month):   **$300,000**

Comparable to the Goodyear blimp, these full-sized airships can be decorated with your name, logo, and artwork on the side, and generally rent for $300,000 to $400,000 per month. The rental charge covers all flying costs, including the use of a pilot. Each airship holds about $45,000 worth of helium. There are only 8 full-size blimps operating in the U.S.
Source: Airship International Ltd., Orlando, FL (407-351-0011)

Hot air balloon: **$18,000**

For a basic model. A larger, 3-burner, $57,000 Thundercolt weighs 11 tons when inflated and holds 10 passengers. Also available are hot air balloons in special shapes—such as the Klondike polar bear and the Etonic running shoe—for about $200,000.
Source: Naturally High Balloon Co., Phoenix, AZ (800-238-6359)

Champagne balloon voyage: **$239**

Per person. Festival Flights, Inc., operates at more than 100 locations worldwide. Champagne is served at the conclusion of the flight—perpetuating a tradition started by the very first balloonists who carried champagne as an offering to puzzled landlords and frightened peasants. Various voyages are available, including the "Sweetheart Balloon Voyage" (for two exclusively) in which the gondola is garlanded with

silk dogwood blossoms and champagne is served aloft. Best time to fly is at daybreak or just before sunset. The company's brochure advises that "during the middle of the day, or any time the sun is 45 degrees or more above the horizon, thermal activity makes the air unstable for ballooning."
Source: Festival Flights, Inc. (800-4-HOTAIR)

40-foot inflatable King Kong balloon: $15,000
Of the kind used in parades.
Source: Southern Outdoor Promotions, Marietta, GA (800-447-6780)

30-foot inflatable Santa Claus balloon: $10,000
Santa's boots are 8 feet long.
Source: Southern Outdoor Promotions, Marietta, GA (800-447-6780)

Ultralight airplane kit: $7,900
Once assembled, the plane weighs 254 pounds, flies at up to 58 mph, can ascend to an altitude of 14,000 feet, and will carry a maximum payload of 241 pounds. More expensive model kits run as high as $18,755.
Source: Quicksilver Enterprises, Inc., P.O. Box 1572, Temecula, CA 92593

World Record Paper Airplane Kit: $10
The book/kit contains 10 different designs, including one that holds the Guinness record for indoor time aloft (17.2 seconds).
Source: Klutz, 2121 Staunton Court, Palo Alto, CA 94306 (415-424-0739)

Pebble from the Moon: $147,500
Three small pebbles from the Moon sold for $442,500 in 1993 at a Sotheby's sale of Russian space memorabilia. At the same auction a Russian Soyuz space capsule brought $1.7 million.

U.S. flag flown to the Moon: **$4,400**

6-inch by 4-inch flag was flown aboard Apollo 11, and
is signed by astronaut Buzz Aldrin. The flag was sold
by Superior Galleries of Beverly Hills at a space memorabilia auction in 1993.

50-foot by 100-foot American flag: **$8,000**

Made of polyester or nylon. Each star on the flag measures 2–3 feet high. The flag weighs 250–300 pounds.
A 200-foot steel pole is needed to display it, and costs
about $30,000 installed. The large flags most com-
monly used at shopping centers and car lots are only
20 feet by 38 feet, and cost $964 in cotton or $858 in nylon. A tapered aluminum 80- to 100-foot pole, costing
$5,500–$7,500 installed, would handle the smaller flag.
Source: American Flag and Pole (800-289-0036) and
Grand Old Shoppe, Amarillo, TX (800-332-3516)

Bargains Galore

A blacksmith's anvil, a straitjacket, and a hand grenade may not have much in common on the surface, but they're all "bargains" in this book.

Ventriloquist's dummy: **$250**

Maher Studios' deluxe 32-inch ventriloquist figure. Select from 24 male and female characters. "All Deluxe figures have full 360-degree turning head, open and close mouth, and side to side (self-centering) eyes." The characters have complete bodies, lifelike wigs, and come outfitted: female figures wear a dress, and male figures wear slacks and sport shirt. Most figures are Caucasian but "any figure can be made with Black, Hispanic, or Caucasian skin colors. . . . All figures are shipped *without* freckles unless you request them." A dummy with an ability to raise its eyebrows is $50 extra. Maher also offers a ventriloquist course—30 illustrated lessons plus cassettes—for $79.95. Further assistance is available with *Give Your Puppet an Accent—Dialect Instruction* audiocassettes, for $16.95 each; 24 separate dialects are available, including Polish, Cockney, and upper-class New England ("Kennedy-esque"). *If the String Breaks* booklet ($3) tells how to handle emergencies.

Source: Maher Studios, Box 420, Littleton, CO 80160 (303-798-6830)

• • •

Blacksmith's anvil (504 pounds): $2,060

British-made, one-piece cast steel with ground and polished face heat-treated and tempered, from Vaughan/Brooks. Anvil measures 40 inches long by 6 ½ inches wide. Anvils are priced more or less according to their weight. An 8-pounder costs only $32. Source: Centaur Forge, Ltd., P.O. Box 340, Burlington, WI 53105-0340 (414-763-8350)

Straitjacket: $189.95

Institutional quality. "Very secure." Source: The Pleasure Chest, 7733 Santa Monica Blvd., West Hollywood, CA 90046

High-wheeler bicycle: $1,029.11

From an original 1870 design. Front wheel has a 48-inch diameter. Bicyclist must have a 28-inch inseam to ride it. Source: Cumberland General Store, Rt. 3, Box 81, Crossville, TN 38555 (800-334-4640)

Perfume-making kit: $29.95

Distillation condenser captures favorite garden fragrances—rose, lavender, lemon blossom, and so on—from raw materials. Instructions explain 5-step distilling process to create homemade perfume. Source: Edmund Scientific Company, 101 E. Gloucester Pike, Barrington, NJ 08007-1380 (609-573-6250)

September 1955 *Playboy* magazine with Marilyn Monroe centerfold: $100

Confederate $1 bill: $35

In average condition. A Confederate $100 bill (almost uncirculated) brings only $95. Confederate bonds can also be bought at a considerable discount to their original face value—for $75 each.

Source: South Carolina Militaria, P.O. Box 104, Columbia, SC 29202-0104

Original movie poster from $5,000
Gone with the Wind (1939):
Source: Kronakos, 9201 Washington St., Denver, CO 80229 (303-457-2612)

Original movie poster from *Jurassic Park* (1993): $20
Source: Kronakos, 9201 Washington St., Denver, CO 80229 (303-457-2612)

Magician's box for sawing a person in half: $4,500
May cost up to $8,500, depending on the options.
Source: Owens Magic Supreme, 734 N. McKeever Ave., Azusa, CA 91702 (818-969-4519)

Magician's cane: $300
Flick the cane and *Presto!*—it instantly turns into a large, colorful bouquet of flowers.
Source: Owens Magic Supreme, 734 N. McKeever Ave., Azusa, CA 91702 (818-969-4519)

Left-handed scissors: $30
At Left Hand World in San Francisco, scissors for the southpaw cost $30 and up. Left-handed versions of wristwatches, rulers, coffee mugs, butter knives, and oven mitts are just a few of the other items found at the store where "the customer is not always right."
Source: Left Hand World, P.O. Box 330128, Pier 39, San Francisco, CA 94133-0128 (415-433-3547)

Yo-yo holster: $8
Tooled black leather yo-yo holster attaches to the belt and keeps yo-yo right at hand. "For the yo-yo aficionado who has everything." Yo-yos themselves range anywhere from $5 for the cheapest plastic models to $75 for models made from aircraft aluminum.

Source: Klutz, 2121 Staunton Court, Palo Alto, CA
94306 (415-424-0739)

Juggling pins (set of 3):   **$30**
Basic juggling clubs are 19 inches long and made of
injection-molded polyethylene. Performance-quality
clubs—advertised as "quick, light and very flashy"—
cost $80 for a set of 3.

Source: Klutz, 2121 Staunton Court, Palo Alto, CA
94306 (415-424-0739)

100 sticks of dynamite: **$140**
1 1/4-inch by 8-inch sticks are 60% nitroglycerin, and
weigh about 1 pound each. For obvious reasons, not
just anyone can purchase dynamite. Purchasers must
have a special license from the Bureau of Alcohol, Tobacco and Firearms, as well as a state permit.

U.S. practice hand grenade: **$7.95**
Cast-steel replicas "Look and feel like the real thing!"
Available in "lemon," "baseball," or "pineapple" styles.
Source: Quartermaster, 750 Long Beach Blvd., Long
Beach, CA 90813 (800-444-8643)

Communications Skills

The ideal form of communication would be ESP—it's cheap, wireless, and unaffected by government regulation. But for those who aren't endowed with psychic abilities, effective communication can be as complex as starting your own TV station (you'll need an FCC license first) or as simple and traditional as having your own U.S. Postal Service–style mail collection box (you can legally own one).

1-hour phone call from Moscow, Idaho, to Moscow, Russia:

$128.09

AT&T's peak-time rate, including tax. Between 2 A.M. and 7 A.M. (Moscow, Idaho, time), the cost is only $98.74 with tax.

3 minutes on the UFO information 900 line:

$5.97

"Sightings, abductions, active UFO areas, theories. . . . - Hear the latest news on these and other topics, or leave YOUR OWN message . . ." $1.99 a minute.
Source: (900-933-UFO1)

Stop the Calls kit:

$3

Guide tells the best ways to halt unwanted telephone solicitations.
Source: Center for the Study of Commercialism, 1875 Connecticut Ave. N.W., Suite 300, Washington, DC, 20009

Wake-up call service in Denver (monthly rate):   **$12**
A friendly voice greets you each morning at the desired time.
Source: Academy Answering Service, Denver, CO
(303-936-8411)

FCC television broadcasting license: **$170**
The fee for a call sign is $55.

Mail collection box (U.S. Postal Service style):   **$600**
Standard drive-up mail deposit box is 20 inches wide,
49 ½ inches high, and 21 ½ inches deep. They're
bought by organizations other than the Postal Service
(utilities, for example, use them as payment drop-off
boxes). Private citizens can buy them too, in any color
other than postal blue.
Source: Gress Corp., 4088 West 63rd St., Chicago, IL
60729 (800-551-5131)

Chinese interpreter in New York City (daily rate):   **$560**
The going rate for an interpreter is about $70 per hour
for most languages, with a usual minimum rate of 2
hours. An exotic language such as Swahili costs $5–$10
per hour more. This is for "consecutive" translation
(the translation *follows* the original remarks). "Simulta-
neous" translators are a little more expensive. Travel
expenses are extra.

Braille "rest room" sign: **$20.30**
This and other Braille safety signs are more than a convenience—they are required in certain buildings and
public areas by the Americans with Disabilities Act.
Source: W. W. Grainger, Inc. (800-225-5994)

• • •

Publishing your own book (1,000 copies)   **$2,167**
with a "vanity" press:
For a 224-page paperback with a 2-color cover. Type-setting is extra ($4–$5 per page). There are also additional charges for manuscript critique, proofreading, and editing. Prices vary, of course, according to length, trim size, binding, and quantity desired.
Source: Professional Press, P.O. Box 4371, Chapel Hill, NC 27515 (800-277-8960)

Get Rich Quick

It's hard to make money without spending some first. For those in a hurry to accumulate wealth, a seat on the New York Stock Exchange may be just the thing. Others with more patience (and a smaller budget) may prefer to subscribe to Benjamin Franklin's dictum that "a penny saved is a penny earned," and purchase, for a fraction of the cost of a seat on the Exchange, a subscription to The Tightwad Gazette.

Seat on the New York Stock Exchange: **$750,000**

Ownership of one of the 1,366 seats on the NYSE entitles the holder to trade stocks on the floor of the exchange. Prices for the seats, like stock shares, can go up or down: the highest price for a seat in 1970 was $320,000; in 1980, $275,000; and in 1993, $775,000.

Nevada casino license: **$2,500**

$2,500 covers the application fee for a "non-restricted gaming license" (needed to operate a full casino) for a corporation with 4 principals. However, in addition to that cost, applicants must pay the Nevada Gaming Control Board's cost of investigating them and doing background checks (easily $50,000 to $100,000). Once approved and in business, the casino owners pay steep annual fees for the number of slot machines and gaming tables in their establishment. Assorted other taxes raise the annual cost of operating a casino even higher. On the other hand, a simple "restricted" gaming license allows drugstores, supermarkets, and similar establishments to have up to 15 slot machines on their premises; it costs only $494 per machine per year.

Cigarette vending machine: $2,000

Soft drink vending machine (can type): $1,200
Deluxe models—which hold up to 500 cans and include, among other features, a dollar-bill validator—can cost up to $3,500.

Soft-serve ice cream machine (single barrel): $8,000
Dispenses 7–8 gallons of ice cream per hour. A double-barrel machine dispenses 2 separate flavors or a twist (2 flavors in 1 scoop), and costs approximately $13,000. In general, soft-serve ice cream machines start at about $4,000 for a low-volume tabletop unit and reach $30,000 for a high-volume machine that has a heat-treated, self-cleaning feature.

Management consulting study by McKinsey & Co.: $1 million
Fortune magazine describes McKinsey & Co. as "the most well-known, most secretive, most high-priced, most prestigious, most consistently successful, most envied, most trusted, most disliked management consulting firm on earth." McKinsey's clients include many of the world's largest corporations, as well as various international governments. The staff of 3,100 consultants is based in 28 countries (starting salary is over $70,000, partners make a couple of million dollars a year), and includes many White House Fellows, Ph.D.s, and Rhodes Scholars. A typical million-dollar study will have 4 or 5 McKinsey consultants working with a client company for 3 to 6 months. A study might focus on one issue, such as whether to add or drop a product line, or could involve the restructuring of an entire company. The end product is a report, usually about 100 pages in length.

Subscription to *The Tightwad Gazette:* $12
Articles by editor Amy Dacyczyn ("The Frugal Zealot") are snappy and informative: "Money-Saving Hobbies" (cutting hair, car maintenance), "Used Shoes, Are They Okay?," "I'm Dreaming of a Tight

Christmas." The "What to do with . . ." department explains how to recycle used pregnancy-test kits ("save several and reuse them as a play chemistry set"), how to make a hammock from plastic six-pack rings ("tie them together with fishing line"), and how to make a wall organizer out of the pockets of old blue jeans. Readers contribute their own money-saving discoveries: for example, one reader wrote in to suggest buying Disney souvenirs at garage sales *before* taking the family to Disney World.

Source: *The Tightwad Gazette,* RR1 Box 3570, Leeds, ME 04263-9710

Grab Bag

A can of worms, a dose of poison, a fake I.D.—this is the rummage sale you've been waiting for!

A Gutenberg Bible:
$4.9 million

A copy of the Bible (the first printed book) was sold at a Christie's auction in 1987 for $4.9 million—the highest price ever paid for a book. Johann Gutenberg printed 180 copies of the Bible between 1450 and 1455; only 48 have survived.

Ticket to George Burns's 100th birthday party:
$100

Three shows are scheduled at Caesars Palace in Las Vegas on 19–21 January 1996, and a fourth on 18 January is expected to be added since the first three shows have already sold out.

Ticket to a Metropolitan Opera performance:
$145

For center parterre box seats during a weekend performance. Less expensive seats in the family circle, for Monday through Thursday performances, cost $21. The cheapest seats in the house (with only a partial view of the stage) cost only $14, Monday through Thursday.

Source: Metropolitan Opera, Lincoln Center, New York, NY 10023 (212-362-6000)

Membership in the Official Madonna Fan Club: $29

A jigsaw puzzle—of yourself: $500

Stave puzzles are "the world's most challenging, most beautiful, handcrafted, personalized jigsaw puzzles." All Stave puzzles are made of wood. They are also quite expensive: an 8-inch by 10-inch puzzle (160 pieces) costs about $500. A 14-inch by 18-inch puzzle (500 pieces) costs $1,500. For a price (up to more than $7,000), Stave can reproduce any design (a personal photo, a Renoir print, original artwork, for instance). One Texas man ordered a puzzle for his girlfriend which, when completed, showed a Victorian bride dressing for her wedding. Across the bottom was printed the question: "Will You Marry Me?" (She said yes.) Stave's regular-style puzzles are difficult enough, but their trick puzzles are renowned for bedeviling the most skilled puzzler. Puzzles with irregular shapes or "phony" corners and border pieces, puzzles that fit together many wrong ways but only one right way, and puzzles with pieces that can fit into more than one place—these are all hallmarks of the Stave trick puzzles. Since almost all Stave puzzles are customized to some degree, delivery usually takes 4–6 weeks. However, the company's brochure suggests that rush orders are a possibility: "Bribery (with peanut M&Ms, of course) has been known to be effective." Stave puzzles, naturally, do not come with box-top pictures.
Source: Stave Puzzles, P.O. Box 329, Norwich, VT 05055 (802-295-5200)

Moving a (1-story) house in Iowa: $4,500

Ron Holland House Moving, Inc., in Forest City, Iowa, estimates the cost of moving a 1-story, 1,000-square-foot house at $4,500 to $6,500. Moving a small 2-story house would cost $8,500 to $10,000. If the house is made of brick, the price doubles. The largest expense isn't the distance a house is transported; it's loading and unloading the house.

• • •

Fumigating a 2,000-square-foot house in Miami: $600

A gas fumigant is used to kill drywood termites and similar pests. The house is then wrapped in canvas tarp for 20 hours. All food, plants, medicines, animals, and, of course, people must be removed. The price quoted is for a house on a concrete slab. Fumigating a vented house (a raised house with a crawl space) is about 30% more.
Source: Bug Busters, Miami, FL (305-233-7222)

Hiring a moving van to move a household from Greenwich, Connecticut to Malibu, California: $16,000

A 48-foot van fully loaded with 30,000 pounds of household goods. Includes transportation, loading and unloading, but not packing. The price works out to about 45 cents a pound. The cost of a move depends on numerous factors. It's especially expensive, on a per pound basis, to move a small load. It could cost $1.50 per pound (about $3,000) to move only 2,000 pounds of household items across country.

Adopting a child: $9,000

The average cost through an adoption agency. Private adoptions usually cost $10,000 to $15,000, including about $4,000 in legal fees.

DNA match (paternity testing): $600

The test covers 3 samples of organic material (blood, cell tissue, hair with root), usually from the mother, the father, and the child. Results are used primarily in court cases to determine parentage. Also used in criminal cases. A forensics DNA match costs $535 per sample. At least 2 samples are usually tested; for example, blood is often taken from a crime scene to have its DNA compared with the DNA of a suspect. DNA matching is regarded as highly reliable; as evidence it usually holds up in court. DNA matching of plant and animal materials is also a thriving business.
Source: Lifecodes, 550 West Ave., Stamford, CT 06902 (203-328-3300)

Aerial photo of your property: $150

Assumes property is within 20 miles of the place where the airplane is based. Otherwise additional mileage charges apply. Includes more than 50 photographs of the property. Photographs can pinpoint a single home site taken from an altitude as low as 1,000 feet, or can cover an area as large as about 1,900 acres. For larger properties, several photos are taken and then pasted together. The plane uses a Global Position Satellite signal to pinpoint the target.
Source: Airphoto—Jim Wark, 5 Belita Drive, Pueblo, CO 81001 (719-542-5719)

Star on the Hollywood Walk of Fame: $5,000

The famous pink granite stars, which are embedded on the sidewalks along a 2 ½-mile stretch of Holly-wood Boulevard and Vine Street, are not free. Celebrities must pay for them. However, each applicant for a star must be approved by various committees. Currently, there are almost 2,000 stars with names on the Hollywood Walk of Fame, and another 300–400 blank stars awaiting a qualified buyer.
Source: Hollywood Chamber of Commerce

English manorial lordship title (average price): $21,000

There is an active and competitive market in the 15,000 to 20,000 recognized manorial titles in England. Prices have risen 1,400% since 1970. However, ownership of a title does not bestow ownership of any land or property, and few of the ancient prerogatives (like collecting taxes) go with the titles. Possessors of the titles can call themselves Lord or Lady of the Manor, and can still shoot game, gather firewood, and fish rivers on "common land." Some particularly attractive titles go for much more than the price quoted here. In 1990, the lordship title of Stratford-upon-Avon (the home of William Shakespeare) sold for a record $228,000.

• • •

Set of the finest bed linens (queen size) at   **$3,690**
D. Porthault of New York:
Top sheet and pillow shams, $1,345; bottom sheet,
$545; two pillow cases, $590; blanket cover, $400; bed
ruffle, $810.
Source: D. Porthault, New York, NY (212-688-1660)

An "alternate I.D.":   **$125**
The "total I.D. package," as advertised in *Soldier of Fortune* magazine, includes an "emergency passport and
two pieces of supplemental I.D. all completely legal."
Another ad in the same magazine offers a passport
with 3 backup photo I.D.s for $400.

Psychological Stress Evaluator (lie-detector test):   **$7,500**
The Psychological Stress Evaluator (PSE) is rapidly replacing the polygraph as the preferred method of lie
detection. The PSE detects stress in voice components.
PSEs have many applications, but under federal law
no lie-detection procedure can be used to screen employees or prospective employees. However, there are
no such restrictions in many other countries. One advantage of the PSE over the polygraph is that the subject does not have to be hooked up to the machine.
Therefore, it can be used to evaluate recorded statements or, for example, the voice of a politician speaking on television.
Source: Dektor Counterintelligence, Savannah, GA
(912-238-0075)

Cyanide (100 grams):   **$43.35**
The average fatal dose for human beings is about 50 to
60 milligrams. Therefore, 100 grams of cyanide is
enough to kill about 1,800 people. Arsenic, another
well-known poison, is less expensive. It costs only $29
per 100 grams, but is considerably less toxic. Bacteria
and toxins are available through companies such as
Merck and Sigma Chemical Co., but, fortunately, they
sell them only to persons who have a legitimate use for
them.

A can of worms (20): $2.60
Adults who have not purchased a fishing worm since
childhood may be surprised to learn they now fetch
more than 10 cents apiece. And they no longer come in
a can, but a Styrofoam cup.
Source: Budget Tackle, Granby, CO (303-887-9344)

Panama Canal toll (average): $32,950
Fees are based on vessel tonnage, but $32,950 is the av-
erage toll paid by each ship that uses the canal. The
canal grosses about $1 million a day. Only about 400 of
the more than 12,000 vessels that pass through the
canal each year are U.S.-based.

Hummer (civilian version of army Humvee): $39,988
The mammoth "jeep" can climb a 60% grade, ford 30
inches of water, and tow 9,000 pounds. Arnold
Schwarzenegger owns one.
Source: AM General Corp., P.O. Box 7025, South Bend,
IN 46634-7025

Polaroid 600 SE professional instant camera: $521
Unlike other Polaroid cameras, the Polaroid 600 SE lets
you select aperture and shutter speed, change lenses,
and use different types of film, including both color
and black-and-white. The price includes the camera
body only. Three interchangeable lenses are available,
costing from $485 to $781 each.
Source: Polaroid Corporation, P.O. Box 100, Penfield,
NY 14526

National public opinion poll: $30,000
National polling organizations, which thrive on pub-
licity, are actually shy about discussing their fees. But
$30,000 to $40,000 will purchase a nationwide poll of
about 1,000 respondents who answer 30 to 40 questions in a 15-minute telephone interview. The pollster
provides full service: helps draft questions, and
processes and analyzes the data. A nationwide survey

with a single question can be purchased as an add-on to a preexisting survey for only about $1,000. An extremely complex and lengthy survey (with, for example, 30 questions and 2,000 to 4,000 respondents) would cost from $75,000 to $125,000.

1 ounce of marijuana: $300
Price depends on quality and difficulties of the marketplace, and can range from $100 to $500 per ounce. *High Times* magazine publishes a monthly state-by-state market report, and even has a 900 phone number for up-to-the-minute market quotes.

Drug test: $25
Quantity discounts are available. A "general screen" tests for drugs of abuse in several classes (barbiturates, THC, amphetamines, opiates). "Thin layer chromatography" ($30–$40) tests for drugs of abuse *and* pharmaceuticals. This test identifies compounds which can then be matched with an identity chart. Workplace drug testing is a growing business: 85% of major companies now test workers and applicants, up from just 22% in 1987.
Source: Evergreen Forensics Lab, Evergreen, CO

Drug test "antidote": $22.99
Naturally Klean Herbal Tea, the Original Quick Flush. "Urine Analysis? Don't Worry! Naturally Klean guarantees desired results in 3 hours."
Source: DJB Sales, Southfield, MI (800-844-8944)

One-Shots

Can you guess what a single M&M costs? How about a bar of motel soap? One square of toilet paper? Or how about one single Frito?

A single mile of interstate highway:
$17.76 million

The cost per mile in 1992 dollars, according to the U.S. Department of Transportation. There is a tremendous difference between the cost of laying highway in a rural area ($8.48 million per mile) and in an urban area ($38.04 million per mile). The whole 42,800 miles of interstate highways has cost some $128.9 billion to build.

1 swordfish:
$765

On a per-pound basis, swordfish is worth more ($3.06, ex-vessel or wholesale price) than salmon. The average swordfish weighs 250 pounds.

A single king (chinook) salmon:
$37.87

The average king salmon weighs 18.9 pounds, and the ex-vessel or wholesale value averages about $2.04 per pound.

1 razor blade:
52.72 cents

Gem razor blades, package of 7 for $3.69.

1 disposable diaper: **32.66 cents**
Huggies disposable diapers, large size (for baby boys,
22–35 pounds), box of 26 for $8.49.

1 plastic trash bag: **24.9 cents**
Glad trash bags, 2 feet 6 inches by 3 feet, 1.01 mil thick,
box of 10 for $2.49.

A single brick: **19.5 cents**
3-hole red building brick.

A single .38-caliber Remington bullet: **19 cents**
A Remington .45 automatic cartridge costs 27 cents,
and a .308 Winchester rifle cartridge costs 45 cents.

1 vitamin C tablet: **11.69 cents**
Nature-Made vitamin C, 1,000 milligrams, with acerola
and bioflavonoids, bottle of 60 tablets for $7.01.

1 extra-strength Tylenol caplet: **9.58 cents**
Bottle of fifty 500-milligram caplets for $4.79.

1 bar of motel soap: **6.34 cents**
$63.40 per case of 1,000—½-ounce Cashmere Bouquet
(wholesale).

A single crayon: **5.2 cents**
Crayola crayons, box of 96 assorted colors for $4.99.

1 tea bag: **5.19 cents**
Box of 48 Lipton tea bags for $2.49.

1 stick of gum: **4.95 cents**
Trident sugarless gum, pack of 18 for 89 cents.

1 generic aspirin tablet: **1.23 cents**
300 tablets, 325 milligrams each, for $3.69 per bottle.

A single wire clothes hanger: **4 cents**
$40.45 per case of 1,000 (wholesale).

1 Bayer aspirin tablet: **3.67 cents**
300 tablets, 325 milligrams each, for $10.99 per bottle.

1 Milk-Bone dog biscuit: **3.43 cents**
Original Milk-Bone brand biscuit, medium size for 20-
to 35-pound dogs, 26-ounce box, 78 biscuits for $2.67.

A single butter pat: **1.3 cents**
90 pats per pound at $1.20 per pound (wholesale).

1 plastic fork: **4.13 cents**
Box of 24 for 99 cents.

1 Q-Tip: **1.17 cents**
Q-Tip cotton swabs in the easy-access dispenser, 170
per package for $1.99.

A single Kleenex tissue: **0.72 cent**
Kleenex facial tissues, 2-ply, 9 inches by 8.4 inches, box
of 175 for $1.25.

1 honey-roasted peanut: **0.59 cent**
12-ounce can of Planters honey-roasted peanuts, con-
taining 441 peanuts for $2.57.

•   •   •

A single M&M:
A 1-pound bag of plain M&M candies for $2.69, containing 502 pieces.

0.54 cent

1 Frito:
Fritos, 11-ounce bag for $1.99, containing 419 chips.

0.48 cent

A single cotton ball:
Crystal brand medium-size cotton balls, package of 600 for $2.29.

0.39 cent

A single rubber band:
Alliance rubber bands, size 12, $^{13}/_{16}$ ounce net weight, 215 rubber bands for 49 cents.

0.23 cent

1 square of toilet tissue:
Charmin, blue, lightly scented, $1.04 for 4 rolls of 1,200 1-ply squares.

0.09 cent

All the . . . and Enough to . . .

All the gold in Fort Knox seems like quite a lot of money until you realize that it amounts to only $211 for each American. And you may be surprised to learn that all the tea in China equals slightly less than $1 for each man, woman, and child in China.

All the gold in Fort Knox:
The U.S. Treasury's stockpile of gold at Fort Knox totals 147.3 million ounces—worth about $373 per ounce.

$54.9 billion

All the tea in China:
Mainland China's annual tea production is about 530,000 metric tons. The value (based on the London auction tea price) is 91.2 cents per pound.

$1.1 billion

All the apples in Washington:
The state of Washington produces about 4.3 billion pounds of apples per year, valued at about 22 cents per pound.

$950 million

• • •

All the electricity used to light the Empire State Building for 1 day: $10,959

The Empire State Building uses 40 million kilowatt-hours per year at a cost of about 10 cents per kilowatt-hour. Since it furnishes power to all the offices in the building, some of the electricity is used for purposes other than lighting.

All the electricity to run Disneyland for 1 day: $19,408

Disneyland's electric bill averages $590,000 a month.

All the bourbon in Kentucky: $1.6 billion

Value of 1 year's production.

All the cattle in Texas: $8.2 billion

There are 13.6 million cattle in Texas (it was only a few years ago that the population of people finally overtook the population of cattle). The cattle are worth an average of $605 per head.

All the oil from 1 Texas oil well (per year): $56,840

Price was calculated from the annual value of Texas crude oil production divided by the 172,607 producing wells in the state. The great majority of these wells aren't big moneymakers. A landowner with wells on his property usually gets a royalty that amounts to a small percentage of the total production. As one rancher put it, "My wells just make enough money to keep me in cigarettes."

All the potatoes in Idaho: $672 million

Yearly production of 6.1 million tons, worth $5.50 per 100 pounds.

All the hogs in Iowa: $1 billion

There are 14.8 million hogs in Iowa, worth $69 apiece.

• • •

All the wheat in Kansas:
Annual production of 363 million bushels at $3.65 per
bushel.

**$1.3
billion**

All the cheese in Wisconsin:
Wisconsin produces nearly 1 billion pounds of cheese
per year, worth about $1.20 per pound.

**$1.2
billion**

All the (common) stock (as of 30 September 1994) of—

—TCBY (The Country's Best Yogurt) Enterprises:

**$147
million**

—Broderbund Software

**$517
million**

—USX-U.S. Steel:

**$3.2
billion**

—Sara Lee:

**$10.8
billion**

—Walt Disney:

**$20.1
billion**

—Wal-Mart:

**$53.7
billion**

All the oranges from 1 Florida orange tree (for 1 year):
Value of the oranges produced by an average tree
(250–350 pounds) during the 1992–93 season. A
bumper crop was produced that season, so prices were
lower than usual. The prior year (1991–92 season) the
value was $16 per tree.

$9

**Enough Scotch tape to circle the earth
at the equator:**
The equatorial diameter of the earth is 24,902 miles.
One roll of Scotch Magic Tape, ½ inch by 108 feet, costs
$1.19. It would take a little more than 1.2 million rolls
of tape to circle the earth.

**$1.4
million**

Enough beer to fill an Olympic-size swimming pool: **$2**
An Olympic-size swimming pool measures 50 meters   **million**
(55 yards) long by 21 meters (23 yards) wide by 1.8 meters (5 feet 11 inches) deep, and holds 504,213 gallons.
Cheap beer costs 99 cents per quart ($3.96 per gallon).

Enough stretch wrap to cover the state of Utah: **$41.1**
A 20-inch by 1,000-foot roll of stretch wrap (90 gauge)   **billion**
costs $29.95. It takes 16,694 rolls to cover a square mile
(about $500,000 worth). The area of Utah is 82,168
square miles. Almost 1.4 billion rolls of stretch wrap
would be needed to cover the entire state.

Enough jet fuel to fly a Boeing 747 from   **$10,024**
New York to Los Angeles:
A 747 uses about 6 gallons of fuel per mile, but jet fuel
costs only about 64 cents per gallon.

Enough fuel for a space shuttle mission: **$2**
The approximate cost of the liquid nitrogen and oxy-   **million**
gen to power the main engines, maneuver the orbiter,
and bring the shuttle back to earth. Not included is the
pair of solid rocket boosters that cost about $76 million
new, but which are refurbished after each mission.

Enough artificial turf to cover a football field: **$109,952**
Based on a field 360 feet long and 160 feet wide. Sta-
dium turf for outdoor fields costs $17.18 per square
yard. Indoor turf is even more expensive—$25.27 per
square yard. The price does not include installation.

Enough tobacco for 1 pack of cigarettes   **11 cents**
(grower's price):
Source: Tobacco Growers Information Committee, Inc.

The Cream of the Crop

The pick of the lot, the crème de la crème, the pièces de résistance. This section is for those who want Lamborghinis instead of Volkswagens, Château Lafite instead of Ripple. Only the very best—or at least the most expensive.

A Lamborghini: **$249,000**
Lamborghini Diablo VT (all-wheel drive) with V-12, 492-horsepower engine. The car accelerates from 0 to 60 mph in 3.9 seconds and has a top speed of 202 mph.

A Ferrari: **$225,500**
Ferrari 456GT, front engine, 2+2 coupe.

The most expensive perfume at Bloomingdale's   **$360**
(1 ounce):
Jean Patou 1000.

The world's biggest rhinestone: **$50,000**
The world's largest rhinestone weighs 115,000 carats (52 pounds), is bigger than a basketball, and currently resides—where else?—at the Liberace Museum in Las Vegas.

• • •

The most expensive diamond: **$12.76 million**
Sold at Sotheby's in Geneva in 1990. The Mouwad Splendour is a 101.84-carat, 11-sided, pear-shaped, mixed-cut diamond. It is the most expensive diamond ever sold at auction.

A suit (off the rack) at Bernini in Beverly Hills: **$2,000**
For an Armani, Zegna, or Cannali.

The most expensive Harley-Davidson motorcycle: **$16,195**
Ultra Classic touring model with 1,340-cc engine weighs 765 pounds. The fully equipped bike comes with cruise control, CB radio, and AM/FM cassette stereo with front and rear speakers. Harley's entry-level motorcycle, the XLH Sportster, weighs 488 pounds and costs $4,900.

The most expensive teddy bear: **$85,000**
A 1920-vintage teddy bear recently sold in England for a record price at auction.

Wedgwood black jasper Portland vase: **$10,000**
The 11-inch vase is the most expensive item in the current Wedgwood line.

The most expensive Item in the Frederick's of Hollywood catalog—silicone breast form "falsies":   **$198**
Per pair. According to the catalog, they "create an entirely new and exciting bustline—the one you've always dreamed of!" A lace-over satin bra with pockets to hold the breast forms costs $26. (By comparison, most items in the 80-page catalog are priced well under $100.)

Nike shoes—Air Force Max CB (Charles Barkley):   **$135**
This and another shoe, the System Ultra (a hi-tech cycling shoe), are at the top of the Nike line at $135 per pair. The average Nike shoe retails for about $70.

The most expensive stamp:
Penny Black, 2 May 1840 cover, sold in 1991.

$2.4 million

The most expensive coin:
1907 U.S. Double Eagle Ultra High Relief $20 gold coin, sold privately in 1990.

$1.5 million

The most expensive bottle of wine:
A bottle of 1787 Château Lafite claret sold at a Christie's auction in Great Britain in 1985. The bottle was engraved with the initials of Thomas Jefferson.

$131,250

An IWC wristwatch:
The International Watch Co. Ltd.'s Grande Complication wristwatch displays time, date, day of the week, month, year, decade, and century, as well as the phases of the moon. The watch has 9 hands and 659 individual parts. It can be set to announce the hour, quarter-hour, and the minute in distinctive gongs. The casing and bracelet are made of hand-finished platinum.

$250,000

A world globe ("The Diplomat") by Replogle:
The illuminated 100-inch-diameter globe is advertised as "the world's most detailed." The globe map is lithographed in 10 colors, its cradle mounting is made of hand-carved mahogany, and the solid brass meridian has hand-engraved numerals. For more limited budgets, Replogle has handsome floor-standing globes for about $200 and up. They're available through Rand McNally Map & Travel Stores.

$5,600

A Waterford crystal world globe:
The large world globe (19 inches high) is the most expensive piece of Waterford crystal available (along with a crystal chess set for the same price). A small world globe (13 inches high) is sold for $3,000.

$12,500

The most expensive glass paperweight: $258,000
One-of-a-kind French paperweight from the 1840s.
(L. H. Selman Ltd. of Santa Cruz, California, conducts
twice-yearly auctions of antique and contemporary
paperweights.)

Comparison Shopping

They say it pays to shop around. Here's the proof.

Video Cassette (VHS) of—

• Oliver Stone's *Wall Street,* starring Charlie Sheen: $14.99

• *Debbie Does Wall Street* (XXX), starring
Candace Heart: $19.99

3,000 gallons of water from—

• the faucet, in Clearwater, Florida: $6.12

• Evian bottled water: $16,934

Average cost for Alka-Seltzer tablets (36) in—

• Manhattan: $5.09

• Washington, D.C.: $3.51

Average cost for 1 pair of pantyhose in—

• Chicago: $5.00

• Boston: $3.16

Average cost to have 1 shirt laundered in—

• Manhattan: $1.87

• Atlanta: $1.16

Strand of pearls—

• **4-strand cultured-pearl choker with 18-karat gold and diamonds, from Tiffany's:** $17,500

• **3-rope pearl choker with crystal and faux platinum clasp from Carolee's Hollywood Glamour collection:** $175

Vitamin C tablet at—

• **the supermarket:** 2 cents

• **the Alta Bates Hospital in Berkeley, California:** $3.09

A pair of crutches—

• **cost to the Humana Group (hospital chain):** $8.35

• **price Humana charged its patients:** $103.65

The vitamin C tablet and the pair of crutches are two examples provided by Jessica Mitford in her 1992 book, *The American Way of Birth*. In fairness to the Humana Group, the 1991 congressional study that was the source of the "pair of crutches" example found that the company's average markup on supplies was only 127%.

A quart of Russian vodka at—

• **a Moscow street market:** $1

• **a liquor store in Chicago:** $6.99

Average cost of a home in—

• **the U.S.:** $118,100

• **Japan:** $346,400

The average home in the U.S. is 1,773 square feet. In Japan, it's 800 square feet.

Cost of a mid-priced car (average) in—

• **the U.S.:** $9,700

• **Norway:** $27,500

Cost of a tooth filling (average) in—

• **the U.S.:** $36

• **France:** $12

Source for home, car, and tooth filling: *Where We Stand*, by Michael Wolff, Peter Rutter, and Albert F. Bayers III, Bantam Books 1992 .

An autographed photo of—

• **Presidents Nixon, Ford, and Carter:** $275

• **The Three Stooges (Curly, Moe, and Larry):** $3,750

Each photo was sold at the same auction in New York City in 1993.
Source: *The Cleveland Plain Dealer*

**$100,000 of term life insurance
(yearly premium) for—**

• **a 60-year-old non-smoking female:** $833

• **a 60-year-old non-smoking male:** $1,111

• **a 60-year-old smoking female:** $1,224

• **a 60-year-old smoking male:** $1,886

• **a 20-year-old non-smoking female:** $148

• **a 20-year-old non-smoking male:** $163

Garden State Life guarantees that policies can be renewed at the same premium for 10 years.

• • •

A 27-inch Zenith stereo TV purchased—

• through "Rent to Own" at Rent-A-Center: **$1,481.22**
Pay $18.99 a week for 78 weeks.

• outright at Sears: **$479.99**

A fast-food meal at—

• Wendy's: **$4.19**
Big Classic combo includes cheeseburger, fries, and a
drink. Drive-through service available.

• the Puppy Hut, a restaurant for dogs, in Toledo, Ohio: **$5**
Includes vegetarian "cheeseburger," fries, and a beef-
flavored drink. Drive-through service available, as well
as dine-in seating. (Puppy Hut's seating is a fenced-in
area called "Park N Bark," with dog-size picnic tables.)

• Hand-knit wool sweater at—

• a duty-free shop in Heathrow Airport: **$90**

• a sweater store in Edinburgh, Scotland: **$65**

Then and Now

The least surprising revelation of this book: prices rise over time. But there are exceptions to every rule. (You should have sold off that IBM stock back in 1987 . . .)

Earl Scheib auto paint job—
- in 1964: $29.95
- in 1994: $149.95

60-second TV ad during the Super Bowl—
- in 1967 (the first Super Bowl): $75,000
- in 1994 (for two 30-second spots): $1.8 million

First-class U.S. postage stamp—
- in 1960:   4 cents
- in 1972:   8 cents
- in 1994:   29 cents

3-minute phone call from New York to Los Angeles (daytime)—

- in 1917: $20.70
- in 1952: $2.50
- in 1994:   75 cents

Copy of the *Chicago Tribune*—
- in 1917:   1 cent
- in 1952:   5 cents
- in 1994:   50 cents

1 pound of round steak—
- in 1890:   12 cents
- in 1930:   43 cents
- in 1970: $1.30
- in 1994: $3.15

1 quart of milk—
- in 1890:   7 cents
- in 1930:   14 cents
- in 1970:   33 cents
- in 1994:   71 cents

Hershey's chocolate bar—
- in 1917:   2 cents
- in 1952:   5 cents
- in 1994:   45 cents

1 ounce of silver—
- in January 1980: $38.27
At its historic peak.
- on 30 September 1994: $5.59

1 share of IBM stock—
- at its 1987 high: $175.90
- on 30 September 1994: $69.63

1 share of Microsoft Corp. stock—
- **at its 1986 high:** $2.80
- **on 30 September 1994:** $56.13

Tuition at the University of Virginia (1 year, in-state)—
- **in 1917:** $20
- **in 1952:** $219
- **in 1994:** $3,880

Movie ticket (national average)—
- **in 1917:** 15 cents
- **in 1952:** 49 cents
- **in 1994:** $5.45

Alexander Calder fish-shaped mobile—
- **in 1942:** $400
- **in 1987:** $187,000
- **in 1993:** $376,500

For the same piece of art, sold three times.

Cézanne painting *Still Life with Apples*—
- **in 1958:** $252,000
- **in 1993:** $28.6 million

On both occasions, the painting was sold at a Sotheby's auction. The 1993 sale is a record price for a Cézanne.

Lunch at the Treasury Department executive dining room—
- **in 1992:** $4.75

Lobster with asparagus and poached pears.

- **in 1994:** $8.50

When Lloyd Bentsen took over, the bargain prices disappeared—as did lobster on the menu.

Federal firearms license (annual cost)—

• in 1992: **$10**

• in 1993 (after passage of the Brady bill): **$66**
At the time the Brady bill was passed in 1993, there were 284,000 licensed dealers in the U.S.—more than the number of gas stations.

Alaska—

• in 1867: **$7.2 million**
When the U.S. purchased it from Russia for 2 cents an acre.

• in 1994: **$36.3 billion**
Appraised value of Alaska real estate today. Includes real property ($20.4 billion) and oil and gas properties ($15.9 billion), but excludes most government-owned land, which constitutes the vast majority of Alaska's total land mass.

Oldies but Goodies

Some notable firsts, some sentimental favorites, a few unsavory prices, and a couple of fateful purchases.

A pair of Levis (circa 1880):   **$1.12**
Riveted Levis were first introduced in 1874. They sold
for $13.50 per dozen.

Price of a slave in 1859:   **$2,000**
For a prime field hand.

First-class passage on the *Titanic* (1912):   **$1,085**
One-way, Southampton to New York City, for a man,
wife, maid, and manservant. Price was for a luxury
suite with cut-glass light fixtures, plush carpeting, and
elegant draperies and furniture; included use of the
gymnasium, the swimming pool, the squash court, a
turkish bath (with masseuse), and a specially stocked
library for first-class passengers only. A one-way
second-class fare could be had for as little as $50.

A ticket to the Beatles' concert in   **$5.65**
Shea Stadium (1965):

•   •   •

A ticket to the Woodstock concert (summer 1969): $6

However, when hundreds of thousands of people showed up, making it impossible to regulate attendance, the promoters declared it a "free concert."

A ticket to the world premiere of $10
***Gone with the Wind* in Atlanta (1939):**

More than 2,000 people attended the 15 December premiere at Loew's Grand Theater.

Admission to the 1929 Academy Awards $5
at the Roosevelt Hotel:

Hula Hoop (1958): $1.98

Within 6 months after Wham-O introduced it in the U.S., 30 million had been sold by the company and its competitors.

First Ford Mustang (1964): $2,368

The sporty car was an instant hit: 700,000 were sold in the 1964–65 model year (a first-year record for any automobile).

First Model T car (1908): $850

In the first year of production, Henry Ford sold 6,000 Model Ts for a price about equal to a teacher's annual salary. By 1916, the price had dropped to $360. That year, 475,000 Model Ts were sold.

A quart of Bacardi rum during Prohibition: $1.50

From a price list issued by an illegal New York liquor shop.

A year's tuition at Harvard in 1814: $300

•　•　•

The first automatic pop-up toaster (1926):   **$12.50**
The Toastmaster Model 1A1, according to a longtime
toaster repairman, contained enough parts to make 5
or 6 modern toasters, and was so well built that many
are still in use today.

First Polaroid camera, Model 95 (1948):   **$89.75**

One-way passage on the *Hindenburg* (1936–37):   **$400**
Air service between Germany and the U.S. took about
60 hours. The *Hindenburg* made 10 round-trip trans-
atlantic crossings before it exploded over Lakehurst,
New Jersey, on 6 May 1937.

The Italian carbine rifle used to kill John F. Kennedy: **$21.45**
Lee Harvey Oswald purchased the rifle by mail in
1963.

Ticket to *Our American Cousin* at Ford's Theater   **50 cents**
in Washington, D.C., 14 April 1865:
For a seat in the dress circle where the presidential box
was located. Ticket prices ranged from 25 cents to $1.

Mississippi poll tax (1920s):   **$2**
In 1923, 38 states had poll taxes. The tax was intended,
in part, to discourage blacks from voting. Poll taxes
were finally banished in the 1960s.

First birth control pill, month's supply (1960):   **$11**

First Barbie doll (1959):   **$3**
Mattel introduced the 11 ½-inch Barbie in 1959. Since
then, her facial features and general appearance have
been updated slightly to reflect changing attitudes toward women.

First transcontinental airfare, one-way (1939):   **$375**
On Pan Am, from New York to Southampton, $675
round-trip. New York to Paris was the same price.

The price of Florida in 1819:   **$5
million**
Spain ceded Florida to the U.S. in exchange for a $5
million credit on its debt to the U.S.

First ballpoint pen (1945):   **$12.50**
Advertised as the "first pen that writes underwater."

First electric blanket (1946):   **$39.50**
Sold by the Simmons Co. of Petersburg, Virginia.

First Apple computer (1977):   **$1,298**
The Apple II—Apple's first fully assembled computer.
It was the first personal computer with an ability to
generate color graphics. However, the Apple II did
not have its own monitor; it was hooked up to a television set.

A pair of eyeglasses in 1785:   **$100**

Truphonic combination phonograph/radio in 1927:   **$187.50**

The first suburban tract houses (in Levittown,   **$7,990
New York, 1947):**
The first homes in America's first major suburb (built
on Long Island farmland 30 miles east of New York
City) were solid 4 ½-room Cape Cod–style bungalows.

· · ·

Stonehenge (1900): $625,000

The historic man-made circle of stones on Salisbury Plain, England, together with 1,300 acres of surrounding land, was offered for sale in 1900. The site was eventually purchased by the British government.

Final Markdown

The cost of all the items in this book: **$635,672,705.03**
This is the total cost of the items in this book. The most expensive is $150 million (renting the space shuttle for a mission) and the cheapest is 0.09 cent (1 square of toilet tissue). (Not counted here are the items in the following sections: "All the . . . and Enough to . . .," "Comparison Shopping," "Then and Now," and "Oldies but Goodies.") Happy shopping!